Aleph Isn't Tough

An Introduction to Hebrew for Adults
Book I

Linda Motzkin

Hara Person, EDITOR

Dedicated to my parents, Drs. Donald and Evelyn Motzkin

Co-Chairs

Jan Katzew

Lawrence Raphael

Hebrew Literacy Task Force

Rick Abrams

Sharon Forman

Dan Freelander

Dru Greenwood

Deborah Joselow

Hara Person

Jamie Rosenberg

Peter Schaktman

Linda Thal

Josee Wolff

Eric Yoffie

Library of Congress Cataloging-in-Publication Data

Motzkin, Linda.
   Aleph isn't tough : an introduction to Hebrew for adults / Linda Motzkin.
      p. cm.
   English and Hebrew.
   Includes bibliographical references (v. 1, last page).
   ISBN 0-8074-0726-7
   1. Hebrew language--Textbooks for foreign speaker--English. 2. Jewish religious
education--Textbooks for adults. I. Title.

PJ4567.3 .M68 2000
492.4'82421--dc21   00-023011

Printed on acid free paper
Copyright © 2000 by URJ Press
Manufactured in Canada

ACKNOWLEDGMENTS

This book owes its existence to the vision of Rabbi Eric Yoffie, President of the UAHC, who, together with Rabbi Sheldon Zimmerman, President of HUC-JIR, issued a call in 1996 for an historic campaign to revive Hebrew literacy throughout the Reform movement. The UAHC Hebrew Literacy Task Force, co-chaired by Rabbis Jan Katzew and Lawrence Raphael, was convened to respond to this challenge. All the members of the Task Force participated in the discussions that led to the decision to create this book, and had a role in developing the book.

Many rabbis, educators, and authorities in the field of Hebrew language instruction and information technology were consulted prior to the writing of this book. The following individuals graciously responded to my questions and shared their experience and expertise. While the orientation of this book may or may not reflect their views, their willingness to engage in dialogue with me was greatly appreciated: Rabbi Bob Abrahamson, Sylvia Abrams, Rabbi Norman Cohen, Rivka Dory, Irving Goldfine, Rabbi Elyse Goldstein, Bina Guerrieri, Aviva Kadosh, Rabbi Doug Kohn, Dr. Avi Lansky, Shlomit Lipton, Lesley Littman, Dr. Alan Mintz, Nechama Moscowitz, Dr. Adina Ofek, Bob Rosin, Baruch Sienna, Cheri Silver, Barbara Spack, and Michael Starr. Rabbis Jonathan Adland and Andrew Sklarz also generously gave feedback and comments at a later point in the process.

Several congregations agreed to pilot the material, and the feedback from the teachers and students of those classes was critical to the shaping of the final book. I am grateful to these congregations, which included Beth Tikvah Congregation, Hoffman Estates, IL; Congregation Emanu-El, San Fransisco, CA; Temple Shaari Emeth, Manalapan, NJ; Temple Adath Israel, Lexington, KY; and Beth Torah Temple, Philadelphia, PA.

A few individuals deserve to be singled out for special thanks. Deborah Eisenbach-Budner and Rabbi Paula Feldstein both offered detailed suggestions and practical advice regarding the teaching of Hebrew to adults. Dina Maiben provided invaluable background information on research related to Hebrew language learning; her article "Issues in Hebrew Reading Instruction" published in *The New Jewish Teacher's Handbook* (ARE) is highly recommended to anyone desiring a clear, easily accessible, yet comprehensive overview of the subject. Rabbi Hara Person, editor of the UAHC Press, originally conceived of many of the special features that appear in this text. She was all that I could have hoped for in an editor and more, providing constructive and timely feedback at every stage of the book's composition.

I also want to thank those who played a role in moving this book from manuscript form into an actual published book. Ken Gesser, Stuart Benick, Michelle Young and Liane Broido all played important roles in this process. Leo Haber, Manya Weg, Debra Hirsch Corman, and Yitzhack Shelomi all lend their considerable talents to this project.

On a personal level, I wish to acknowledge my mentor in the field of adult Hebrew language instruction, Ethelyn Simon. And, above and beyond all the praises I could utter is my colleague and life's partner, my co-rabbi and husband, Jonathan Rubenstein, who not only proofread every jot and tittle of this book, but assumed a disproportionate share of our shared responsibilities to enable me to write. Without his assistance, and the support and patience of our children, Rachel, Ari, and Shira, this book could simply not have been written.

INTRODUCTION

To the Student

There is a mystical teaching that the entire universe and all it contains was fashioned out of the letters of the Hebrew alphabet. When the Holy One spoke and the world came to be, it was through the combining of letters into words and words into speech that Creation occurred. Therefore, the letters and vowels of the Hebrew alphabet are more than symbols printed on a page. They provide an opening into new creative possibilities, new levels of understanding, and new worlds of experience. We congratulate you on your decision to begin this study and wish you much satisfaction as your knowledge increases.

To the Teacher

This book is the first step in a program of Hebrew learning for adults. It introduces the letters and vowels of the Hebrew alphabet in a carefully selected sequence, with the goal of developing the student's ability to phonetically sound out any vocalized Hebrew text.

How is this book different from all other beginning Hebrew books? Each chapter of this book contains additional information—besides the introduction of five or six new phonetic symbols—designed to broaden the student's exposure to and understanding of the workings of the Hebrew language. Thus, each chapter contains:

- one or two Jewish concept words, chosen from among the most well-known classical Hebrew vocabulary
- one Hebrew root, chosen from among those that appear most frequently in the Bible or prayer book
- a key phrase from Jewish religious life and/or a key quote from the Bible or liturgy that utilizes either the new Hebrew root or one of the concept words
- examples of modern and classical Hebrew words formed from the chapter's new Hebrew root
- prayer book excerpts utilizing various forms of the chapter's new Hebrew root
- a list (in the latter half of the book) of Hebrew words frequently encountered in contemporary Jewish life, composed of the letters and vowels already learned
- a concluding section containing a short explanation of a concept related to Hebrew learning, such as *gematria*, trope, midrash, or an element of grammar

This additional information is intended to engage and inform the student and to enrich the classroom learning experience; however, memorization and mastery of all this material are not necessary at this introductory stage. You may use your discretion in determining how much of this additional material to incorporate into a given class session.

For additional information on this text and its use in the classroom, we encourage you to consult the Teacher's Guide published as a companion to this volume.

There are twenty-two letters in the Hebrew alphabet. In this chapter, three are introduced:

Bet (with a dot)	**b** as in **b**oy	בּ
Shin	**sh** as in **sh**ip	שׁ
Tav	**t** as in **t**ie	ת

Reading Practice

Say aloud the sound of the following letters. Try to do it without looking at the chart above. Hebrew is read from right to left, so begin at the right side of the page.

ת בּ שׁ ת שׁ ת בּ ת שׁ בּ ←

In English, the letters of the alphabet represent both consonant sounds (b, c, d, f, etc.) and vowels (a, e, i, o, u). In Hebrew, the letters represent consonant sounds, while vowels are indicated by symbols that are written above, below, or beside the letters. In this chapter, we introduce two vowel symbols that are written below the Hebrew letters. These two symbols indicate the same sound:

sounds like **ah** as in **fa**ther	◌ַ *(The ◌ַ represents any Hebrew letter.)*
sounds like **ah** as in **fa**ther	◌ָ *(The ◌ָ represents any Hebrew letter.)*

When reading letters with vowels, sound the consonant first, then the vowel. Examples:

בָּ   Sound the *b* first, then the *ah*, to produce *ba*.

שָׁ   Sound the *sh* first, then the *ah*, to produce *sha*.

Reading Practice

Read aloud the following letter and vowel combinations. Remember to read from right to left.

← .a שָׁ שָׁ שָׁ שָׁ תָ בַּ תָ שָׁ בֵּ בָּ בְּ שָׁ תַ

In both Hebrew and English, a syllable can consist of a single consonant and a single vowel, as in the line of Hebrew above. A syllable can also consist of a consonant-vowel-consonant combination, such as in the words *bat* or *tot* in English.

Read aloud the following consonant-vowel-consonant combinations. Each should be pronounced as a single syllable. Remember to read from right to left.

← .b שַׁב שָׁשׁ שָׁשׁ בָּשׁ תָּת תַּת בַּת שָׁת

.c בָּב תַּב בָּת תָּת תָּשׁ שָׁשׁ שָׁב

Longer combinations can be read by sounding out the individual syllables. Remember that some syllables will consist of just a consonant and a vowel, while others will be consonant-vowel-consonant combinations. Example: בָּתָשׁ.

The first syllable is a consonant and a vowel—*ba*.

The second syllable is a consonant-vowel-consonant combination—*tash*.

Together, they would be sounded as *ba-tash*.

Last syllable gets the accent

Read aloud the following combinations. Remember to read from right to left.

← .d בָּתָת בַּת בַּת בָּ תָּת שָׁתָת תָּת שָׁת שָׁ

.e שָׁבָשׁ בָּשׁ שָׁב בְּ בָּב בָּ בֵּב בָּ

.f תַּתָשׁ תָּת תָּת תַּבָשׁ בָּשׁ בָּ תַּב תַּ

.g (שָׁבָּת) בָּת שָׁב שָׁב שָׁשׁ שָׁ בְּשׁ בָּ

Congratulations! You have read your first Hebrew word. The last word you read on the line above is *Shabbat*: שָׁבָּת.

Shabbat, the Sabbath day of rest, is a cornerstone of Judaism. This word is useful because it incorporates all the Hebrew letters and vowels introduced in this chapter.

The Fourth Commandment

HEBREW Key Quote

Shabbat is the subject of the fourth of the Ten Commandments. See if you can pick out the word *Shabbat* in the Hebrew of the Fourth Commandment. There is an additional Hebrew letter attached as a prefix to the word.

זָכוֹר אֶת־יוֹם הַשַּׁבָּת לְקַדְּשׁוֹ:

Remember the Sabbath day and keep it holy. (Exodus 20:8)

THE ROOT ש-ב-ת

Most Hebrew words are built around a combination of three letters called a root. Many different words can be formed from the same root by changing the vowels, or adding prefixes or suffixes. Words that share the same root have related meanings, all connected in some way to the meaning of the root.

The three letters ש-ב-ת are the root of the word שַׁבָּת. The root ש-ב-ת means "rest" or "cease from labor" or "desist." Notice that there is no dot in the root letter ב. Dots are not written in letters when indicating the root.

The following are examples of Hebrew words formed from the root ש-ב-ת. This book has not yet introduced all of the letters and vowels that appear in these words. Nonetheless, you can see that they all contain the root letters ש-ב-ת with various vowels, prefixes, and suffixes and that they all have related meanings. The letter ב can appear with or without the dot in words that are formed from this root.

cessation	שֶׁבֶת
Sabbath observance; complete rest	שַׁבָּתוֹן
Sabbath rest; *in modern Hebrew: a strike*	שְׁבִיתָה
to stop or put an end to; to lock out	לְהַשְׁבִּית
lockout; cessation	הַשְׁבָּתָה
he ceased work, he rested	שָׁבַת

The following are several prayer book excerpts containing the root ת-ב-שׁ or the word שַׁבָּת. You may already be familiar with the words or melodies of these prayers, though this book has not yet introduced most of the Hebrew letters and vowels which appear in them. Perhaps your teacher or a friend can sing these prayer book excerpts to you. See if you can find the word שַׁבָּת or the root letters ת-ב-שׁ in each excerpt. In some cases, prefixes are attached. The number of occurrences of the root in each excerpt is indicated in parentheses.

The blessing for lighting Shabbat candles (1 occurrence)

בָּרוּךְ אַתָּה יְיָ אֱלֹהֵינוּ מֶלֶךְ הָעוֹלָם, אֲשֶׁר קִדְּשָׁנוּ בְּמִצְוֹתָיו,
וְצִוָּנוּ לְהַדְלִיק נֵר שֶׁל שַׁבָּת.

L'chah Dodi (1 occurrence)

לְכָה דוֹדִי לִקְרַאת כַּלָּה. פְּנֵי שַׁבָּת נְקַבְּלָה.

V'shamru (Exodus 31:16–17) (3 occurrences)

וְשָׁמְרוּ בְנֵי יִשְׂרָאֵל אֶת הַשַּׁבָּת, לַעֲשׂוֹת אֶת הַשַּׁבָּת
לְדֹרֹתָם בְּרִית עוֹלָם: בֵּינִי וּבֵין בְּנֵי יִשְׂרָאֵל אוֹת הִיא
לְעוֹלָם, כִּי שֵׁשֶׁת יָמִים עָשָׂה יְהוָֹה אֶת הַשָּׁמַיִם וְאֶת הָאָרֶץ,
וּבַיּוֹם הַשְּׁבִיעִי שָׁבַת וַיִּנָּפַשׁ.

Vay'chulu (Genesis 2:1–3) (2 occurrences)

וַיְכֻלּוּ הַשָּׁמַיִם וְהָאָרֶץ וְכָל צְבָאָם: וַיְכַל אֱלֹהִים בַּיּוֹם
הַשְּׁבִיעִי, מְלַאכְתּוֹ אֲשֶׁר עָשָׂה, וַיִּשְׁבֹּת בַּיּוֹם הַשְּׁבִיעִי, מִכָּל
מְלַאכְתּוֹ אֲשֶׁר עָשָׂה: וַיְבָרֶךְ אֱלֹהִים אֶת יוֹם הַשְּׁבִיעִי
וַיְקַדֵּשׁ אֹתוֹ, כִּי בוֹ שָׁבַת מִכָּל מְלַאכְתּוֹ, אֲשֶׁר בָּרָא אֱלֹהִים
לַעֲשׂוֹת:

Some students find it helpful when learning the Hebrew letters to write them. The simplest way to write the letters is to use block print, as follows:

בּ בּ שׁ שׂ תּ ת

Block printing is not the form of writing commonly used in Israel or by those who are literate in Hebrew, however. Instead, a script form of each letter, often quite different in appearance from the print form, is used. It is sometimes difficult for beginning students of Hebrew to learn script, since it involves learning two different forms for each letter. This book will present both the block and script forms for each letter. You may choose whichever form you wish to learn and use when writing Hebrew.

These are the script forms of the letters you have learned:

תּ ת שׂ שׁ בּ בּ

Hebrew Writing Exercises

1. Write a line of the letter *Bet*, using either block print or script.

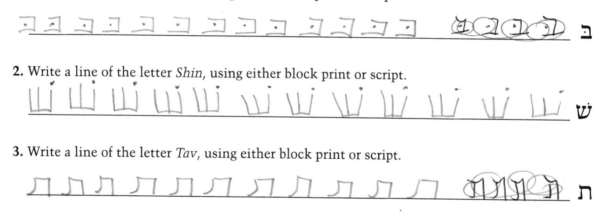

2. Write a line of the letter *Shin*, using either block print or script.

3. Write a line of the letter *Tav*, using either block print or script.

Exercises

1. Read aloud the following letter and vowel combinations. Circle the ones that sound like the English word *tut*.

בַּשׁ (תָּת) (תֵּת) תֵּב בַּת בְּב שֵׁב

2. Read aloud the following letter and vowel combinations. Circle the ones that sound like the English word *shot*.

בַּב בָּת (שָׁת) שֵׁב (שָׁת) תַּת תֵּב תָּשׁ

3. Read aloud the following letter and vowel combinations. Circle the ones that sound like the name *Bob*.

(בָּב) תָּת בַּת בָּשׁ בַּת (בָּב) שָׁב תָּב

4. Read aloud the following letter and vowel combinations.

בָּב שֵׁב שָׁשׁ תַּשׁ בַּשׁ בַּ תָּ שָׁ a.

תָּתָשׁ תָּת תַּת בַּת שָׁת שֶׁ בְּ b.

בָּתָת בַּתָשׁ בַּת בַּת בֵּב בֵּבָ c.

תַּבָּת תַּבָשׁ תֵּב תָּשׁ תַּת תַּ תָּ d.

שֵׁשׁ שַׁבָּשׁ שַׁבָּת שֵׁב שֵׁת שַׁ שֶׁ שֵׁ e.

בָּשׁ בֵּב תָּב תַּבָשׁ תַּתָשׁ תַּת תָּ f.

שָׁתָת שֵׁשָׁת שַׁשׁ שַׁשׁ שַׁשׁ שָׁ תַּ בָּ g.

בֵּבָשׁ שַׁבָשׁ שָׁתָשׁ שָׁת שַׁת שֵׁשׁ שָׁ h.

שַׁבָּת שָׁב תֵּב שָׁב תַּב בָּב בָּ i.

EXTRA CREDIT

Ashkenazic & Sephardic

There are two different systems of Hebrew pronunciation encountered today: Ashkenazic and Sephardic. The Ashkenazic pronunciation was used by the Jews of Eastern and Central Europe, in countries such as Germany, Hungary, Poland, and Russia. The Sephardic pronunciation was used by the Jews of the Mediterranean regions, including Spain, Greece, and North Africa.

Until the middle of the twentieth century, most American synagogues used Ashkenazic Hebrew pronunciation, as the majority of American Jews were of Ashkenazic descent. After the creation of the State of Israel in 1948, however, there was a gradual shift in American congregations toward using Sephardic Hebrew, since that is the standard pronunciation used in Israel. This book teaches Sephardic Hebrew, which is used today by most North American congregations.

One can still hear both Ashkenazic and Sephardic pronunciations used when referring to certain holidays, prayers, or life-cycle events, as in the following examples. (The accented syllable is written in **bold letters**.)

Sephardic Pronunciation	Ashkenazic Pronunciation	Written Form
Shab**bat**	**Shab**bos	שַׁבָּת
Bat Mitzvah	Bas **Mitz**vah	בַּת מִצְוָה
Shavu**ot**	Sha**vu**os	שָׁבְעוֹת
Suk**kot**	**Suc**cos	סֻכּוֹת
Sim**chat** **To**rah	**Sim**chas **To**rah	שִׂמְחַת תּוֹרָה
Yitga**dal** v'yitka**dash**	Yis**ga**dal v'yis**ka**dash	יִתְגַּדַּל וְיִתְקַדַּשׁ

The two types of Hebrew are identical in their written forms. It is only their pronunciation that distinguishes them. Notice that Sephardic Hebrew words are generally accented on the last syllable, while Ashkenazic Hebrew words are generally stressed on the second-to-last syllable. Sephardic Hebrew does not distinguish between the two vowels ▊ and ▊, introduced at the beginning of this chapter (pronouncing both of them as *ah*) while in Ashkenazic Hebrew ▊ is pronounced as *ah* and ▊ as *aw*. Sephardic Hebrew does not distinguish between תּ and ת, pronouncing them both as *t*. In Ashkenazic Hebrew, the letter ת is pronounced like a *t* when it has a dot in the middle (תּ), and like an *s* when it does not have the dot (ת).

Review

You now know three Hebrew letters: תּ, and בּ, and שׁ.

And you have learned two vowel symbols: ◻ָ and ◻ַ.

Together, these letters and vowels can spell the Hebrew word שַׁבָּת.

rest, cease from labor, desist — שׁ-ב-ת

This chapter introduces two new letters: *Lamed* and *Mem*. *Mem* is one of five Hebrew letters that have two different forms: a regular form, used at the beginning or in the middle of a word, and a final form, used only as the last letter of a word.

Lamed	l as in lake	לְ
Mem	m as in mom	מ
Mem Sofit (Final Mem)	m as in mom	ם

Reading Practice

Say aloud the sound of each of the following letters, which include those from the last chapter as well as the new letters. Try to do it without looking at the chart above.

a. ← ל מ ם ם ב לְ שׁ ם ם ת לְ ם ם

Read aloud the following letter and vowel combinations.

בַּ בָּ שָׁ שַׁ תַ תָ מָ מַ לֵ לַ .b

מַ לָ שָׁ תָ לַ מָ בַ לָ שָׁ מָ .c

Mem Sofit (Final *Mem*) is only used as the last letter of a word. It appears in the following line as the last letter of each consonant-vowel-consonant combination. Remember that a consonant-vowel-consonant combination forms a single syllable. Read this line aloud.

מָם לַם מַם תַם לָם שָׁם בָּם .d

Read aloud the following single-syllable combinations.

לָשׁ מָשׁ מַם תַם תַל שָׁל מָל בַּל .e

מַב לַב מָשׁ לָשׁ מַם לַם מָת לַת .f

Read aloud the following longer combinations of letters and vowels. Remember to sound out the individual syllables. Each syllable is either a single consonant with a single vowel or a consonant-vowel-consonant combination.

בְּמָל בְּלָל בַּבְל בָּב בַּל בְּמָ בָּם .g

מָלָל תָלָל תָמֶם תָמָ מַמָ תָמָ תָם .h

שָׁבָל שַׁבָּם שְׁמָם שָׁלֵם שָׁל שָׁמָ שַׁם שָׁם .i

לָבֶּם לְמֶם לְמָ לָת לָתָשׁ לָבָשׁ לָשׁ .j

In this chapter, two new vowel symbols are introduced. One is written next to the Hebrew letter and the other is written to the upper left of the Hebrew letter. Both indicate the same vowel sound:

sounds like **o** as in flow	וֹ␣ (The ␣ represents any Hebrew letter.)
sounds like **o** as in flow	␣ֹ (The ␣ represents any Hebrew letter.)

Reading Practice

Read aloud the following letter and vowel combinations.

שׁוֹ שׁ לוֹ ל תוֹ ת מוֹ מ בּוֹ בּ .a

ל שׁ מוֹ בּ לוֹ ת מ ל שׁוֹ תוֹ .b

לוֹם בֹּם תֹם מֹם שׁוֹם תוֹם שֹׁם בֹּם .c

שֹׁת בּוֹת מֹת מל תֹּל בֹּל שׁוֹל מוֹל .d

When the vowel ◌ֹ is followed by the letter שׁ, only one dot is used for both the letter and the vowel. When the vowel וֹ is followed by the letter שׁ, each has its own dot.

לשׁ תוֹשׁ תשׁ בּוֹשׁ בֹּשׁ מוֹשׁ מֹשׁ .e

You have now learned the letters and vowels that spell another basic Jewish vocabulary word: שָׁלוֹם.

This is the Hebrew word *shalom*, for "peace." It is also used as a greeting, equivalent to the English words *hello* and *good-bye*. It can be combined with the word *Shabbat*, the vocabulary word you learned in the last chapter, to produce the phrase שַׁבָּת שָׁלוֹם.

This is the traditional Shabbat greeting, expressing the hope that all may enjoy "a Sabbath of peace," a peaceful Shabbat.

Psalm 34:15

The Hebrew word for "peace" often appears in the Bible and in our prayer book. See if you can find the word for "peace" in this verse from the Biblical Book of Psalms.

סוּר מֵרָע וַעֲשֵׂה טוֹב, בַּקֵּשׁ שָׁלוֹם וְרָדְפֵהוּ:

Turn from evil and do good; seek peace and pursue it. (Psalm 34:15)

The word שָׁלוֹם ("peace") comes from the three-letter root: שׁ-ל-ם. This root has the basic meaning of "completion" or "wholeness." The word שָׁלוֹם, therefore, means more than just an absence of warfare and violence. It implies a wholeness, a lack of fragmentation, a spiritual completeness.

There are many expressions in Jewish life that utilize the word שָׁלוֹם or the root שׁ-ל-ם. In addition to the Sabbath greeting שַׁבָּת שָׁלוֹם, there is the expression *refu'ah shleimah*, "a complete healing," which one wishes to those who are ill: רְפוּאָה שְׁלֵמָה. (This book has not yet introduced all the letters and vowels in these words, but you can recognize the root letters שׁ-ל-ם. When suffixes are attached and the root letter ם is no longer the last letter of the word, *Mem* appears in its regular form, מ.)

The following are other examples of Hebrew words formed from the root שׁ-ל-ם. This book has not yet introduced all of the letters and vowels that appear in these words. However, you can see that they all contain the root letters שׁ-ל-ם with various vowels, prefixes, and suffixes, and that they all have related meanings.

complete, whole, perfect	שָׁלֵם
to be completed, finished	לִשְׁלֹם
to pay, recompense; to complete; to discharge a commitment	לְשַׁלֵּם
to make peace, reconcile; to complete, acccomplish	לְהַשְׁלִים
fulfilled, perfect	מְשֻׁלָּם
completeness, wholeness, perfection	שְׁלֵמוּת
Solomon (Shlomo)	שְׁלֹמֹה

The following are prayer book excerpts containing the word שָׁלוֹם. You may already be familiar with the words or melodies of these prayers, though this book has not yet introduced most of the Hebrew letters and vowels appearing in them. Perhaps your teacher or a friend can sing these prayer book excerpts to you.

Try to find the word שָׁלוֹם in each excerpt. (The number of occurrences in each excerpt is indicated in parentheses.) In some cases, prefixes made up of other Hebrew letters are attached. And in some cases, suffixes are added and the final letter ם is no longer the last letter of the word. When this occurs, the final letter ם becomes a regular מ.

Oseh Shalom (2 occurrences)

עֹשֶׂה שָׁלוֹם בִּמְרוֹמָיו הוּא יַעֲשֶׂה שָׁלוֹם עָלֵינוּ וְעַל כָּל
יִשְׂרָאֵל, וְאִמְרוּ אָמֵן:

Shalom Aleichem (7 occurrences)

שָׁלוֹם עֲלֵיכֶם, מַלְאֲכֵי הַשָּׁרֵת, מַלְאֲכֵי עֶלְיוֹן, מִמֶּלֶךְ מַלְכֵי
הַמְּלָכִים, הַקָּדוֹשׁ בָּרוּךְ הוּא.
בּוֹאֲכֶם לְשָׁלוֹם, מַלְאֲכֵי הַשָּׁלוֹם, מַלְאֲכֵי עֶלְיוֹן...
בָּרְכוּנִי לְשָׁלוֹם, מַלְאֲכֵי הַשָּׁלוֹם...
צֵאתְכֶם לְשָׁלוֹם, מַלְאֲכֵי הַשָּׁלוֹם...

Shalom Rav (4 occurrences)

שָׁלוֹם רָב עַל יִשְׂרָאֵל עַמְּךָ תָּשִׂים לְעוֹלָם, כִּי אַתָּה הוּא
מֶלֶךְ אָדוֹן לְכָל הַשָּׁלוֹם. וְטוֹב בְּעֵינֶיךָ לְבָרֵךְ אֶת עַמְּךָ
יִשְׂרָאֵל, בְּכָל עֵת וּבְכָל שָׁעָה בִּשְׁלוֹמֶךָ. בָּרוּךְ אַתָּה יְיָ
הַמְבָרֵךְ אֶת עַמּוֹ יִשְׂרָאֵל בַּשָּׁלוֹם.

These are the block print forms of the Hebrew letters and one of the vowels introduced in this chapter. (The other vowel introduced in this chapter is written in both block print and script as a dot to the upper left of the Hebrew letter.)

וֹ ו ם מ ל לַ

And these are the script forms of the same letters and vowel.

וֹ ו ם מ ל לַ

Hebrew Writing Exercises

1. Write a line of the letter *Mem*, using either block print or script.

_____ מ

2. Write a line of the letter *Mem Sofit* (Final *Mem*), using either block print or script.

_____ ם

3. Write a line of the letter *Lamed*, using either block print or script.

_____ ל

4. Write a line of the new vowel, using either block print or script.

_____ וֹ

Exercises

1. Draw a line connecting each Hebrew consonant and vowel combination with the English word that has the same sound.

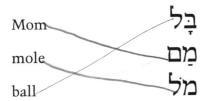

Mom   בָּל

mole   מֶם

ball   מֹל

bomb   תָּם

toll   בָּם

Tom   תוֹל

2. Write the Hebrew consonant and vowel combinations that sound like the following English words. There is more than one possibility for each word.

a. moat _____

b. boat _____

c. bowl _____

_____

_____

_____

d. shoal _____

e. tome _____

f. lobe _____

_____

_____

_____

g. lob _____

h. lot _____

_____

_____

3. Read the following letter and vowel combinations, and circle the sound-alikes in each line.

a. לָל לֹל לַש לֹש לֶש לָלֶש לֹלֹש לַלוֹש

b. בֹל בָל בָלֶל בַּבֹל בָּבֹול בַּבֶל

c. שַׁל שֶׁל שֵׁל שֹׁל שֹׁלוּ שֹׁלָם שוֹל

d. מֶל מֹל מֹלוּ מָלוֹ מָלוֹם מוֹל מֹלָם

e. תָּם תוֹם תוֹמֶת תוֹמוּ תוֹמָם תמוּ

f. שוֹם שֶׁם שֶׁם שָׁמָם שָׁמוֹם שָׁמוּשׁ שֶׁם

4. Read aloud the following letter and vowel combinations.

a. תָ תָשׁ בַּשׁ בֹּשׁ שׁוֹשׁ שׁוֹשָׁשׁ

b. בַּ בֹּשׁ בֹּשׁ מֹשׁ מֹשׁוּ מוֹשׁוֹת

c. תַּת תוֹת תוֹתוּ תוֹתַת שׁוֹתַת

d. בַּת מַת מֹת לוֹת לוֹם לוֹמוּ לָם

e. מוֹם מוֹת מוֹמֵת בּוֹמֵת בְּמָשׁ בָּשׁ

f. שָׁל שֶׁל שׁוֹל שׁוֹלֵם שָׁלוּ שָׁלוֹם

g. תָּל תַּשׁ תּוֹשׁ תּוֹשֵׁל תּוֹשָׁל שַׁשׁ

h. בּוּ בּוֹם שׁוֹם שׁוֹמֵם שׁוֹלֵם שָׁלָשׁ

i. בּוֹשׁ בּוֹשֵׁשׁ בָּשׁוֹשׁ מָשׁוֹשׁ מָשֵׁשׁ

j. שֵׁב שָׁם שָׁבַב שָׁמָם שָׁמוֹם שָׁלוֹם

k. מָשׁ בָּשׁ מְבָשׁ מַבּוֹשׁ מוֹבָשׁ מַשׁ

l. לוֹת לוֹתוֹת לוֹמוֹת לוֹמֵת לוֹמַשׁ

m. בּוּ בּוֹת בּוֹתֵת בּוֹתַת בָּלֵת בַּלָת

n. מַבָּת שַׁבָּת שַׁבָּתוֹת שֵׁמוֹת שָׁמוֹם

EXTRA CREDIT

Appearances of the Letter Shin

The letter שׁ, or the word שַׁדַּי (Shaddai) for which it stands, appears on every mezuzah scroll. The word שַׁדַּי (Shaddai) is one of the names for God, usually translated as "Almighty." Some say the word שַׁדַּי on the mezuzah is an abbreviation for the phrase שׁוֹמֵר דְּלָתוֹת יִשְׂרָאֵל, "guardian of the doors of Israel."

The letter שׁ also appears on the tefillin boxes worn by some Jews during daily morning prayers. Rabbi Lawrence Kushner, in his book *The Book of Letters*, shares the following teaching regarding the שׁ on the tefillin:

I have learned of a tradition recounted in the thirteenth-century Kabbalistic text, סֵפֶר הַתְּמוּנָה, *Sefer Ha-Temunah*. It teaches that one letter is missing from our present Hebrew alphabet and that this letter will only be revealed in the future. The anonymous author goes on to explain that every defect in our present universe is mysteriously connected with this missing letter—an unimaginable consonant whose sound will create undreamed-of words and worlds, transforming repression into loving. You may already have noticed that on either side of the black leather *tefillin* box which is worn on the forehead during morning prayers are raised letter *shin*s. If you look closely, you will notice that one of them (the one on the left side), instead of having three prongs, has four. It looks something like this: שׁ.

Some suspect that this may be the missing letter whose name and pronunciation must wait for another universe. Yet, nevertheless, every morning, we wear it right between our eyes!

Review

You have now learned the following Hebrew letters.

מ סופית   מ   ל   תּ   בּ   שׁ
ם   מ   ל   תּ   בּ   שׁ

toe

You have learned four vowel symbols that represent two vowel sounds.

וֹ   ֹ   and   ַ   ָ

And you have learned two basic Jewish vocabulary words: שַׁבָּת and שָׁלוֹם. These two words can be combined to form the Sabbath greeting: שַׁבָּת שָׁלוֹם.

HEBREW ROOT Review

complete, whole	— שׁ־ל־ם
rest, cease from labor, desist	— שׁ־ב־ת

Root words leave out dots

This chapter introduces two new letters: *Hei* and *Reish*. The letter *Reish* is pronounced by native speakers of Hebrew in the back of the throat in a way unlike any English letter. Most English speakers find it easiest to pronounce the *Reish* like an English *r*.

| Hei | **h** as in hat | (Hey) הַ |
| Reish | **r** as in road | ר (rrr) |

Reading Practice

Say aloud the sounds of the following letters, which include those from previous chapters as well as the new letters. Try to do it without looking at the chart above.

a. ר ה ל ר ה מ ה ר ס ה ר ה ב

b. ר ל ה ת ר ס ש ה ת ל מ ר ם

Read aloud the following letter and vowel combinations.

.c רְ רַ הָ הֶ רֹ רוֹ הוֹ הֹ ה ל מ שׁוֹ בּ

.d הַ רְ שָׁ הָ לְ רַ בָּ הָ תַ רָ מָ לַ

.e הֹ בּ רוֹ תָ מ הֹ ה לוֹ רֹ שׁוֹ הוֹ רֹ

Read aloud the following single-syllable combinations.

.f הֹם רום לֹם רֹם מוֹם שֹם הוֹם בּוֹם

.g הָר בַּר מָר לָר לֹם הָם רַם רַת הַת

.h שָׁר שׁוֹר הוֹר הֹר הַל הֹ שׁ הַם רֶשׁ

In English, the letter *h* at the end of a word is generally not pronounced. For example, the name *Sarah* is pronounced the same way as *Sara* without an h at the end. Similarly, in Hebrew, the letter ה at the end of a word is generally not pronounced. תָה sounds the same as תָ.

Read aloud the following sylables. Remember that a ה at the end is not pronounced.

.i רָ רָה לָ לָה שָׁה בָּה מֶה מֹה רֹה

The following lines contain longer combinations of letters and vowels for you to read aloud. Remember to sound out the individual syllables.

.j רָם רְמָה רוֹמָה רוֹמֶם רְמֶם רְמוֹם רם

.k הוֹל הֹל הַלָל הָלוֹל הָהֹל הָהוֹל הוֹלָל

.l בָּה בָּשׁ בָּשָׁה בּוֹשָׁה הַבָּשָׁה הַבּוֹשׁ

.m תָר תוֹר תָתוֹר תָתָר תָרָה תוֹרָה

Dots in Hebrew Letters

Dots often appear in Hebrew letters and serve various grammatical functions. In most cases, the dots do not affect the pronunciation of the word. There are, however, three Hebrew letters whose pronunciation is altered by the appearance of a dot in the letter. (One of these is the letter בּ, which has a different sound when it is written as ב.) You will learn more about these letters in later chapters. From this point on, the reading practice and exercises in this book will include some letters with dots that do not affect the pronunciation.

The word *Torah* is generally written in Hebrew with a dot in the letter ת: תּוֹרָה.

This basic Jewish vocabulary word has a range of meanings. The Hebrew word literally means "instruction," "teaching," or "law." *Torah* is the name given to the first five books of the Hebrew Bible, contained in the sacred scroll read in the synagogue as part of services on certain days. (The scroll itself is called a *Sefer Torah*—"a Torah scroll.") The word *Torah* is also used more broadly to encompass the central texts of Jewish sacred literature: the entire Hebrew Bible is sometimes referred to as the "Written Torah," while the Talmud is called the "Oral Torah." In its broadest meaning, the word *Torah* is used to refer to the totality of Jewish teaching and learning, including both the commentaries and insights of previous generations as well as our own.

HEBREW Key Quote

Berachot 63b

The word *Torah* appears frequently in Jewish sacred literature, and the study of Torah is an avenue for interaction with others. Notice that in the following quote from the Talmud, the word *Torah* has a prefix attached.

אֵין הַתּוֹרָה נִקְנֵית אֶלָּא בַּחֲבוּרָה.

Torah (knowledge) is not gained except in the company of others. (Berachot 63b)

In this chapter, we introduce three new vowel symbols, two of which are written beneath the Hebrew letter. The third vowel is written with symbols both beneath the Hebrew letter and to the left of the letter.

sounds like **eh** as in bed	*eh* ֶ	(The ⬜ represents any Hebrew letter.)
sounds like **a** as in play (see note on next page)	*a* ֵ	(The ⬜ represents any Hebrew letter.)
sounds like **a** as in play	י *a* ֵ	(The ⬜ represents any Hebrew letter.)

Shack eefes

Note: *Sephardic Hebrew has some variations in pronunciation. One variation concerns the pronunciation of the vowel ⬚. In North America, the vowel ⬚ is generally treated as identical to the vowel יֵ, as indicated in the chart above. In Israel, however, the vowel ⬚ is often pronounced as eh, like the vowel ⬚.*

Reading Practice

Read aloud the following letter and vowel combinations.

You have now learned the letters and vowels that spell another basic Jewish vocabulary word: שֵׁם.

This is the Hebrew word for "name." It often appears in the Bible and in the prayer book in passages that make reference to the name of God.

From the Bible and the prayer book

See if you can find the Hebrew word for "name" in the following quotes. The biblical quote is the third of the Ten Commandments. The quote from the prayer book is the line that immediately follows the six words of the *Shema*.

From the Bible:

לֹא תִשָּׂא אֶת שֵׁם יְהֹוָה אֱלֹהֶיךָ לַשָּׁוְא.

You shall not swear falsely by the name of the Eternal your God. (Exodus 20:7)

From the prayer book:

בָּרוּךְ שֵׁם כְּבוֹד מַלְכוּתוֹ לְעוֹלָם וָעֶד.

Blessed is the name of God's glorious majesty for ever and ever.

THE ROOT ש-מ-ר

You have now learned the Hebrew letters that form a commonly used root: ש-מ-ר. This root has the meaning "guard" or "keep" or "preserve." The phrase שׁוֹמֵר שַׁבָּת, which you can now read and which includes this root, means "guardian (or keeper) of Shabbat," a term used to describe those who maintain a strict level of Shabbat observance. The root ש-מ-ר also appears in the well-known biblical quote from Genesis 4:9:

"Am I my brother's keeper?" הֲשֹׁמֵר אָחִי אָנֹכִי

The following are other examples of Hebrew words formed from the root ש-מ-ר. This book has not yet introduced all of the letters and vowels appearing in these words. Nonetheless, you can see that they all contain the root letters ש-מ-ר with various vowels, prefixes, and suffixes and that they all have related meanings.

guard, keeper	—	שׁוֹמֵר
guarding	—	שְׁמִירָה
watch, shift	—	מִשְׁמֶרֶת
guard, post	—	מִשְׁמָר
conservative, conserving, preservative	—	מְשַׁמֵר
conserved, tinned, canned	—	מְשֻׁמָּר
guarded, reserved, restricted	—	שָׁמוּר
Samaria (Shomron)	—	שׁוֹמְרוֹן
Hashomer Hatzair (name of a Zionist youth group); *literally:* the young guard	—	הַשׁוֹמֵר הַצָּעִיר

The following are prayer book excerpts containing the root ש-מ-ר. You may already be familiar with the words or melodies of these prayers, though this book has not yet introduced most of the Hebrew letters and vowels that appear in them. Perhaps your teacher or a friend can read or sing these prayer book excerpts to you.

Try to find the root ש-מ-ר in each excerpt. (The number of occurrences of the root in each excerpt is indicated in parentheses.) In some cases, the vowel ו appears between two root letters. And in some cases, prefixes and suffixes are attached.

From *L'chah Dodi* (1 occurrence)

שָׁמוֹר וְזָכוֹר בְּדִבּוּר אֶחָד, הִשְׁמִיעָנוּ אֵל הַמְיֻחָד.

Yism'chu (1 occurrence)

יִשְׂמְחוּ בְמַלְכוּתְךָ שׁוֹמְרֵי שַׁבָּת וְקוֹרְאֵי עֹנֶג.

V'shamru (Exodus 31:16) (1 occurrence)

וְשָׁמְרוּ בְנֵי יִשְׂרָאֵל אֶת הַשַּׁבָּת, לַעֲשׂוֹת אֶת הַשַּׁבָּת לְדֹרֹתָם בְּרִית עוֹלָם.

Priestly Benediction used by parents to bless their children (Numbers 6:24–26) (1 occurrence)

יְבָרֶכְךָ יְיָ וְיִשְׁמְרֶךָ.

יָאֵר יְיָ פָּנָיו אֵלֶיךָ וִיחֻנֶּךָּ.

יִשָּׂא יְיָ פָּנָיו אֵלֶיךָ וְיָשֵׂם לְךָ שָׁלוֹם.

PRACTICE Writing

These are the block print forms of the Hebrew letters and one of the vowels introduced in this chapter. (The other vowels introduced in this chapter are simply written in both block print and script as dots beneath the Hebrew letters.)

יִ י ִ ר ר ה ה ה

These are their script forms.

יִ י ִ ר ר ֿה ה

Hebrew Writing Exercises

1. Write a line of the letter *Hei,* using either block print or script.

ה _____

2. Write a line of the letter *Reish,* using either block print or script.

ר _____

Exercises

1. Draw a line connecting each Hebrew consonant and vowel combination with the English word that has the same sound.

rail	רֵיה	home	הַת	
ray	רָת	let	לֶת	
rot	מֶת	hello	הֹם	
met	רֵיל	hot	הֲלוֹ	

2. Write the Hebrew consonant and vowel combinations that sound like the following English words. There may be more than one possible combination.

a. bet _____   **b.** roam _____   **c.** wrote _____

_____   _____

d. rate _____   **e.** roll _____   **f.** hole _____

g. hail _____   h. hate _____   i. robe _____

_____   _____   _____

j. rob _____   k. hem _____   l. hello _____

a. bet _____   c. wrote _____

3. Read aloud the following rhyming combinations.

a. הֵל בֵּל מֵל שֶׁל תֵּל הֲדֵל הַלֵל

b. רֹה לֹוה הֲלֹוה שְׁלֹו בְּלֹו מְלֹו תְּלֹו

c. רֵיה מֵי שָׁמֵי תָּמֵי מָלֵי מֵרֵי הֲרֵי

d. הֵם שֵׁם שֹׁומֵם בֹּושֵׁם לֹומֵם הֹולֵם

e. רֹה שָׁמֹה שָׂרָה שְׁלָה שָׁבָה בָּמֹה

4. Read aloud the following letter and vowel combinations.

a. הַר הֹור הָהָר הַהֹור הַבָּר הַבֹּור

b. שֵׁם הַשֵּׁם רָשֵׁם רֹושֵׁם רֹושֶׁת רֶשֶׁת

c. מֵר שָׁמֵר שֹׁומֵר שֹׁמֶרֶת שָׁמֹור שֹׁור

d. לֵיל לֵילָה הַלֵּל הֵילָה הֵלֹו הֲלָל

e. רֹו רֹום רֹומֵם רֵם רֵמָם רֵמָה

f. תֹּורָה הֹרָה מֹורָה מֹורֶה שֹׁותָה שֹׁותָה

g. בֵּית בֵּיתָה בֵּיתֹו בֵּיתָם בֶּתֶר

h. שֶׁל שֶׁלֹו שָׁלָה שֶׁלָהֶם שָׁלֹם שָׁלֵם

i. רֵם רֹום רֹומָה רֹומֵם רַמָה מָרֹום

j. תָּלָה תָּלֹה תָּלֹות תָּלִי תָּלַל תָּלֵל

k. הֵמָם הַמֵּם הַמֹּול הֵמָה הַמָּל הֵם

l. מַרֵה מָרָה מָרֹום מָרֶם מֵרֶם מֵר

m. בָּבֶל בָּשֵׁל בֹּושֵׁל בָּשֶׁלֶת בֹּושֶׁת

n. מֹות שֵׁמֹות לֵילֹות הַלֵּילֹות הַשֵּׁמֹות

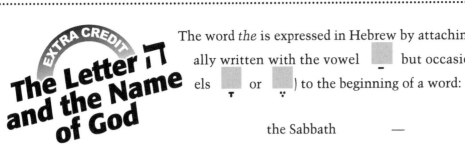

EXTRA CREDIT

The Letter ה and the Name of God

The word *the* is expressed in Hebrew by attaching the letter ה (usually written with the vowel ◌ַ but occasionally with the vowels ◌ָ or ◌ֶ) to the beginning of a word:

the Sabbath	—	הַשַׁבָּת
the Torah	—	הַתּוֹרָה
the name	—	הַשֵׁם

The letter ה is also used in some written texts as an abbreviation for the four-letter name of God, יְהֹוָה. This most sacred name of God is never pronounced; the general practice is to substitute the Hebrew word *Adonai* for this unpronounceable name. In fact, the vowels that accompany the letters יהוה in printed texts are the vowels of the word *Adonai*, not the original vowels of the Divine Name. Many scholars believe that the original pronunciation of the Divine Name was *Yahweh*; there are several Hebrew names and phrases that support this possibility. For example, the name of the prophet Elijah in Hebrew is *Eliyahu*, which means "My God is *Yah*." And the word *Halleluyah*, often translated as "Praise God!" actually means "Praise *Yah*!"

Some suggest that the letters יהוה form a verb from a Hebrew root meaning "to be" or "to exist." *Yahweh* then means "One who causes to be" or "One who brings into existence," a fitting name for the Source of All. The Hebrew word *Adonai* has a different meaning: it literally means "my Lords," though it is generally rendered in English translation as "Lord." (The plural formulation of the Hebrew *Adonai* may have been utilized, like the royal "we" in English, to emphasize God's majesty. It also may be understood to indicate that, while God is One, we experience the Divine in a variety of different ways.)

In the prayer book, the symbol יְיָ is generally used to represent the four-letter name of God and is usually pronounced as *Adonai*. Some Jews use the pronunciation *Adonai* only when actually engaged in prayer, otherwise using the term *HaShem* ("the name," הַשֵׁם) to refer to God. In English translations, there is a variety of different approaches used for translating יְיָ. Some prayer books use "Lord," others use "Eternal," while others use the Hebrew *Adonai* or *Yah* spelled out in English letters. Some use a variety of different attributes of God in the translation of the Divine Name, such as "Merciful One," "Source of Life," and "The Omnipresent." And in place of the grammatically masculine *Adonai*, some substitute the feminine word שְׁכִינָה, *Shechinah*, which in the Jewish mystical tradition represents the indwelling presence of God.

CHAPTER 4

Review

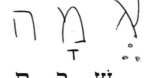

You have now learned the following Hebrew letters.

ר ה מ מ ל ת ב שׁ

You have learned seven vowel symbols, which represent four vowel sounds.

And you have learned four basic Jewish vocabulary words.

שֵׁם תּוֹרָה שָׁלוֹם שַׁבָּת

HEBREW ROOT Review

rest, cease from labor, desist	—	שׁ-ב-ת
complete, whole	—	שׁ-ל-ם
guard, keep, preserve	—	שׁ-מ-ר

This chapter introduces three new letters. The letter *Nun*, like the letter *Mem* which you have already learned, is one of the five Hebrew letters that have both a regular form and a final form. The letter *Aleph* is silent; if it is written with a vowel, only the vowel sound is pronounced. The letter *Ayin* is also regarded as silent by most Hebrew speakers, and that is how we present it in this book. There are, however, some speakers of Hebrew who pronounce the *Ayin* as a guttural sound in the back of the throat, unlike any English consonant.

נ

Nun	**n** as in **n**ame	נ
Nun Sofit (Final *Nun*)	**n** as in **n**ame	ן
Aleph	silent	א
Ayin	silent	ע

Reading Practice

Say aloud the sound of the following letters, which include those from previous chapters as well as the new letters. Say the word "silent" for those new letters that are silent. Try to do this without looking at the chart above.

a. נ ן א ה ע ה נ ן ר א ר נ ן ע ע ס נ ל

b. ן מ א ת ר ע נ ן שׁ א בּ ע

Read aloud the following letter and vowel combinations. When the letter *Aleph* or *Ayin* appears with a vowel, only the vowel sound is pronounced.

c. אָ עַ א עוֹ אִ אֵי עֱ עָ נוֹ אֲ נ נֵ נִי

d. נֶ אֱ עֲ בְּ נ לֵ אַ שָׁ תֵּי עֲ הֵי רֵ

e. נוֹ מֹ אוֹ ל עִי רֵי נ הֶ אָ מֵ עוֹ

Read aloud the following single-syllable combinations.

f. אֵין נֶן הֶן רֵין עוֹן רן תוֹן שֵׁן לֵין

g. מֶן תֶּן נֵן נָר נָה נַל נן הוֹן אוֹן מן

h. עַם נָם עִין בֵּין אַל אָה עַל עוֹר

Read aloud the following longer combinations of letters and vowels.

i. נֵמָה נָמָן הַמָּן הָרָן רָנָן רָנוֹן רוֹנֵן רָן

j. עֵינֵי עֲרִי עָרָר עוֹרֵר עוֹרֵל עָרֵל עָרֵם

k. לֵאָה רֵאָה רִאָה רוֹאָה רָאָה רָעָם רַע

l. שָׁעָה שָׁעוֹן הַשָּׁעוֹן שַׁבָּתוֹן שָׁאַן שָׁאַל

In this chapter, we introduce one new vowel symbol, which is written beneath the Hebrew letter.

silent **OR** *a short sound—* *see explanation below*	▪ *(The* ▪ *represents any Hebrew letter.)*

The ▪ vowel is sometimes silent and sometimes pronounced. When it is pronounced, it has a short indistinct vowel sound like the *a* in *alone* or the *o* in *occur*. Some find it easiest to think of the ▪ vowel simply as a silent vowel that nonetheless requires the sounding of the consonant written above it.

At the Beginning of a Word

When the ▪ vowel appears at the beginning of a word, it has a short sound that enables the consonant above it to be pronounced. Read aloud the following examples.

לָמֶה בְּמֶה בִּמֵי שְׁמֵא שְׁנֵי שְׁנַת בְּנֵי

At the End of a Word

When the ▪ vowel appears under the last letter of a word, it is silent. Read aloud the following examples. The first three consist of just a single syllable.

מַתְ אַתְּ נַתְ נָתַתְּ הָרַתְ בָּאתְ

In the Middle of a Word

When two ▪ vowels appear side by side in the middle of a word, the first ▪ vowel is silent (like the ▪ vowel at the end of a word), and the second is pronounced with a short sound (like the ▪ vowel at the beginning of a word). Read the following line aloud.

תַּל מְרוּ תַּלְמְרוּ תַּשׁ לְמֵי תַּשְׁלְמֵי

When a single ▪ vowel appears in the middle of a word, it is generally silent, although there are instances when it is pronounced with a short sound. Unless you are told otherwise, it is probably best to treat a single ▪ vowel in the middle of a word as silent. Read the following aloud.

שָׁמְרָה שְׁמֶנָה שִׁמְנוֹן שַׁמְרוֹן שׁוֹמְרוֹן

There is one exception worth noting here to the general statement given above. When a single ▢ vowel appears in the middle of a word under a letter that is immediately followed by the same letter, the ▢ vowel has a short sound to enable the pronunciation of both letters. בּוּלוֹ does not sound the same as בּוּלְלוֹ because, in the latter word, a short vowel sound is inserted after the first ל to enable the pronunciation of two ל sounds.

Read the following aloud.

מוֹלְלָה שׁוֹמְמוֹת שָׁתְתָה רוֹמְמוּ שׁוֹלְלָה

Reading Practice

Read aloud the following various combinations containing the ▢ vowel.

.a   הָרֵי בָּרָא מָלֵא נְמֵי נְשֵׁי תְּרֵי תְּלֵי

.b   תִּשְׁמְרוּ שָׁרְרוּ שָׁמְרוּ שָׁרוּ שְׁמוּ

.c   מַתְּתֵי מַתְּנַת בְּנַת מְנַת מְנֵי בְּנֵי

.d   לַמְּן לְמַעַן לְמָן לְאָן לְעַם

.e   אַרְנִי אַרֵי מְאוֹרֵי נְאֵרֵי נָאוֹר נְאוּ

.f   תִּשְׁמְמִי שׁוֹמְמוּ שָׁמַמְתָּ שָׁמַתְּ שְׁמָם

.g   עוֹרְלוּ עוֹרְרוֹת עוֹרְרָה עוֹרְלוֹת עוֹרְלָה

.h   אָנְנָם אַמְנוֹן אַלְמָנָה אַלְמוֹן אַלְמָן

.i   תִּלְבְּשׁוּ תִּלְבְּשִׁי נִלְבְּשׁוּ נִלְבַּשׁ אֶלְבַּשׁ

You have now learned the letters and vowels that spell another basic Jewish vocabulary word:

שְׁמַע

This is a command form of a verb from the root שׁ-מ-ע. The basic meaning of this root is "hear" or "listen" or "obey." The command שְׁמַע can be translated as: "Hear!" or "Listen!" The word שְׁמַע is the first word of the biblical verse Deuteronomy 6:4. This verse is considered the central affirmation of Jewish faith. It is recited during morning and evening services, and some Jews recite it every night at bedtime. It is also part of the text inscribed on the scroll within the mezuzah that hangs on the doorposts of Jewish homes and institutions.

The *Shema*—Deuteronomy 6:4

This verse affirms the Jewish belief in the Eternal One. You may already know the *Shema* by heart. You can now read many of the Hebrew letters and vowels in this verse.

שְׁמַע יִשְׂרָאֵל יְיָ אֱלֹהֵינוּ יְיָ אֶחָד.

Hear, O Israel: the Eternal One is our God, the Eternal God alone!

You have now learned the three letters that form נ-ת-ן, another very common Hebrew root. Its basic meaning is "give," though in some contexts it can mean "grant" or "permit."

The following are examples of Hebrew words formed from the root נ-ת-ן. When the letter נ is the first letter of a root, it sometimes does not appear in words formed from that root. In some of the examples below, the first נ of the root has dropped out and only one ת and one נ remain.

This book has introduced many, but not all, of the letters and vowels that appear in these words. Remember that if a suffix is attached and the final root letter ן is no longer the last letter of the word, it will appear as a regular נ.

present, gift	—	מַתָּנָה
negotiations, "give and take"	—	מַשָׂא וּמַתָּן
given; datum	—	נָתוּן
data	—	נְתוּנִים
given, allowed, permitted	—	נִתָּן
Nathan (*meaning:* He gave)	—	נָתָן
Jonathan (*meaning:* God gave)	—	יוֹנָתָן

The following are prayer book excerpts that contain words from the root נ-ת-ן. You may already be familiar with the words or melodies of these prayers, though this book has not yet introduced many of the Hebrew letters and vowels appearing in them. Perhaps your teacher or a friend can read or sing these prayer book excerpts to you.

Try to find the root נ-ת-ן in each excerpt. (The number of occurrences of the root in each excerpt is indicated in parentheses.) In one case, the first root letter נ has dropped out. In one case, the vowel וֹ appears between two root letters. And in two cases, prefixes are attached.

From the Torah service (1 occurrence)

בָּרוּךְ שֶׁנָּתַן תּוֹרָה לְעַמּוֹ יִשְׂרָאֵל בִּקְדֻשָּׁתוֹ.

Blessing before the Torah reading (2 occurrences)

בָּרוּךְ אַתָּה יְיָ אֱלֹהֵינוּ מֶלֶךְ הָעוֹלָם, אֲשֶׁר בָּחַר בָּנוּ מִכָּל
הָעַמִּים וְנָתַן לָנוּ אֶת תּוֹרָתוֹ. בָּרוּךְ אַתָּה יְיָ, נוֹתֵן הַתּוֹרָה.

From the Torah service (1 occurrence)

יְהֹוָה מֶלֶךְ, יְהֹוָה מָלָךְ, יְהֹוָה יִמְלֹךְ לְעֹלָם וָעֶד. יְהֹוָה עֹז לְעַמּוֹ יִתֵּן
יְהֹוָה יְבָרֵךְ אֶת עַמּוֹ בַשָּׁלוֹם.

These are the block print forms of the Hebrew letters introduced in this chapter. (The vowel introduced in this chapter is simply written in both block print and script as two dots beneath the Hebrew letter.)

שׁ עַ אָ אַ ןּ ן נּ נ

These are their script forms.

אָ עַ אָ אָ ן ן נּ נ

Hebrew Writing Exercises

1. Write a line of the letter *Nun*, using either block print or script.

נ
_____

2. Write a line of the letter *Nun Sofit* (Final *Nun*), using either block print or script.

ן
_____

3. Write a line of the letter *Aleph*, using either block print or script.

א
_____

4. Write a line of the letter *Ayin*, using either block print or script.

ע
_____

Exercises

1. Draw a line connecting each Hebrew consonant and vowel combination with the English word that has the same sound.

English	Hebrew		English	Hebrew
lane	מֵיא		nosh	לֹן
knob	שֹׁן		err	תּוֹא
may	עֶת		aim	נַשְׁ
or	נַבְּ		toe	נֹע
ate	הֶן		ebb	נֵיה
shone	נוֹת		neigh	עָר
note	לֵין		loan	אֶם
hen	אוֹר		know	אֲבְ

2. Write the Hebrew consonant and vowel combinations that sound like the following English words. There may be more than one possible combination.

a. bone _____ **b.** bane _____ **c.** moan _____

_____   _____   _____

d. men _____ **e.** ten _____ **f.** net _____

g. not _____ **h.** name _____ **i.** rain _____

_____   _____   _____

j. own _____ **k.** on _____ **l.** ale _____

_____

3. The following are Hebrew words and names that you may already know. Read each word aloud and connect it to its English equivalent below.

English	Hebrew		English	Hebrew
Moshe (Moses)	לֵאָה		Menashe	תָּמָר
Leah	שְׁלֹמֹה		Rosh Hashanah	עַמְרָם
amen	מְנוֹרָה		Amram	רֹאשׁ הַשָּׁנָה

Shlomo (Solomon)   אָמֵן   Tamar   מְנַשֶּׁה

menorah   מֹשֶׁה

4. Read aloud the following letter and vowel combinations.

a. אַלּוֹן   אֵלֶה   אֶלָּא   אַלָּה   אָלֵם   אֵלֶם

b. עַם   נֶעְלָם   הָעָלָם   הָעוֹלָם   עוֹלָם   עָלַם

c. עוֹנוּ   עוֹנֵנוּ   עוֹנְּה   עוֹנֵן   עוֹנֶה   עוֹנָה

d. הַנֵּרוֹת   נֵרוֹת   נִרְאֶה   נוֹרָא   נֵרוֹא   נֵר

e. מִמַּלְאוֹת   מְמַלֵּא   לְמַלֵּא   מְלֵא   מָלֵא

f. בּוֹנֵן   בּוֹנְנָה   בָּנֵנוּ   בָּנוֹ   בּוֹנֶה   בּוֹנֶה

g. שֵׁנָן   שְׁנָתוֹן   שְׁנַת   שָׁנָה   שָׁנָה   שֵׁן

h. לָשׁוֹן   שׁוֹנֵן   שׁוֹנָה   שׁוֹנַת   שָׁנַן   שֵׁנָן

i. אוֹתָם   אֵיתָן   אַתֶּן   אַתֶּם   אַתָּה   אַתְּ

j. תְּנִי   תְּאֵנָה   תְּנָא   נְאוֹת   נָאֶה   נָאֶה

k. תַּלְמִידָה   תַּלְמָן   תֶּלֶם   תֵּימָן   תְּהוֹם

l. עוֹרְבוּ   עוֹרוּ   עוֹרְרוּ   עוֹרֵר   עוֹר

5. Read aloud the following words taken from the prayer book.

a. לְעֵלָּא   עָלְמֵי   לְעָלַם   רַבָּא   שְׁמֵהּ

b. לְעוֹלָם   בָּעוֹלָם   הָעוֹלָם   עוֹלָם   עַל

c. לְאוֹת   הַלֵּילוֹת   לְהַלֵּל   הַהַלֵּל   הַלֵּל

d. שְׁמַע   שְׁמוֹ   שֵׁם   בֵּין   בּוֹרֵא   אַשְׁרֵי

e. מָרוֹם   הַנּוֹרָא   נוֹרָא   אוֹרָה   תּוֹרָה

f. שׁוֹשַׁנַּת   שֵׁשֶׁת   שָׁמוֹר   שׁוֹמְרֵי   שֶׁל

g. הָאֵלֶּה   אָמֵן   עַמּוֹ   עַם   לְמַעַן   בַּעַל

In English, the letters of the alphabet are often used in place of numbers when making lists or outlines. *A* indicates the first item and represents the number one, *B* represents two, and so forth. Similarly, in Hebrew the letters of the alphabet are often used as numbers.

In the system of Hebrew numerology known as *gematria*, each letter of the Hebrew alphabet has a corresponding numerical value. (There are various ways to establish this correspondence; in the most common system, the first ten letters of the alphabet have the numerical values of 1 through 10; the next nine letters have the values of 20 through 100, and the remaining three letters have the values of 200, 300 and 400 respectively.) Every Hebrew word, therefore, has a numerical value that can be obtained by adding up the values of the individual letters in the word. Words with equivalent numerical values are thought to have some hidden significant connection, and thus *gematria* has been used as a means for discovering secret or esoteric meanings in verses of Scripture.

Individual letters of the Hebrew alphabet are thought to possess certain mystical qualities and attributes, based in part on their numerical value and on the words associated with or beginning with each letter. The letter אֵ is the first letter of the Hebrew alphabet, and hence its numerical equivalent is the number one. Because of its numerical value of one, the letter אֵ is associated with the Holy One. This association is reinforced by the fact that the letter אֵ is the first letter of the words אֱלֹהִים (God) and אֲדֹנָי (*Adonai*) and אֶחָד (one). It is also the first letter of the phrase אֶהְיֶה אֲשֶׁר אֶהְיֶה ("I will be what I will be"), which is the divine name revealed to Moses at the burning bush in Exodus 3:14.

The sound of the letter אֵ is the sound of silence. Some suggest that this is why the letter אֵ is the first letter of the first word of the Ten Commandments: אָנֹכִי יְהוָֹה אֱלֹהֶיךָ ("I am the Eternal your God"; Exodus 20:2). The Divine Revelation at Mount Sinai began with אֵ, with the silent awe that precedes speech. As one midrash describes it:

When the Holy One gave the Torah, no bird chirped, no fowl flew, no ox lowed... the sea did not roar, creatures did not speak, the whole world was hushed into breathless silence, and the voice went forth

אָנֹכִי יְהוָֹה אֱלֹהֶיךָ

"I am the Eternal your God." (Exodus Rabbah 29:9)

Review

You have now learned the following Hebrew letters.

ש ב ת ל מ ם מ ה ה ר א ע נ ן

You have learned eight vowel symbols.

And you have learned five basic Jewish vocabulary words.

שַׁבָּת שָׁלוֹם תּוֹרָה שֵׁם שְׁמַע

rest, cease from labor, desist —	שׁ-בּ-ת
complete, whole —	שׁ-ל-ם
guard, keep, preserve —	שׁ-מ-ר
give, grant, permit —	נ-ת-ן

This chapter introduces two new letters: *Kaf* and *Chet*. The letter *Kaf* is one of the five Hebrew letters that have both a regular form and a final form. *Kaf* is also one of the three Hebrew letters whose pronunciation is altered by the appearance or absence of a dot in the middle of the letter. In this chapter, we introduce the letter *Kaf* without a dot in the middle. The letter *Kaf* without a dot in the middle is pronounced exactly the same as the letter *Chet*. Their sound is not like any consonant in the English language. It is a gutteral sound, like the sound of the *ch* in the name of the German composer Bach.

Kaf (without dot)	**ch** as in Ba**ch**	כ
Kaf Sofit (Final *Kaf*)	**ch** as in Ba**ch**	ך
Chet	**ch** as in Ba**ch**	ח

CHAPTER 5

Look-Alike Letters

Some Hebrew letters have similar shapes and appearances and can be easily confused with one another. Look carefully at the following pairs of look-alike letters.

The letters *Chet* and *Hei* are nearly identical in appearance, except for the space between the left leg and the top bar in the letter *Hei*, which is closed in the letter *Chet*. You might remember this difference between the letters *Hei* and *Chet* by noting that the letter *Hei*, which sounds like *h*, has a **h**ole at the top.

ה   ח

The shapes of the letters *Chet* and *Tav* are also very similar, distinguished mainly by the curving toe at the bottom of the left leg of the *Tav*, while the left leg of the *Chet* is completely straight. You might remember this difference by noting that the letter *Tav*, which sounds like *t*, has a **t**oe.

ת   ח

The letters *Kaf* and *Bet* are often mistaken for one another, especially because both letters can be written with or without the dot inside. Thus far, this book has introduced only the pronunciation of the with a dot inside it and the without the dot. For now, in the reading exercises of this book, the two letters can be distinguished by the presence or absence of the dot. The letters can also be distinguished by the fact that the *Kaf* has a curved shape, while the *Bet*, which sounds like *b*, has a **b**ottom **b**ar that extends **b**eyond the **b**ack of the letter.

בּ   כ

Some confuse the letters *Kaf* and *Nun*, or *Kaf Sofit* (Final *Kaf*) and *Reish*, because they have similar shapes. The letter *Kaf*, however, is much wider than the letter *Nun*. And the letter *Reish* is shorter than the *Kaf Sofit*, which drops down below the line of print. The letter *Reish* can also appear in any position within a word, while the *Kaf Sofit* can appear only as the last letter.

ר   ן   נ   כ

Reading Practice

Say aloud the sounds of the following letters, which include those from previous chapters as well as the new letters. Say the word "silent" for those letters that are silent. Try to do this without looking at the chart on the previous page.

.a ע ת ח נ כ א כ ר ב כ ה ח

.b ם ש ה ח ת מ כ ן ר ח ל

Read aloud the following letter and vowel combinations.

.c נְ כֶ חֲ כֵ חֵי חֶי בֹ כֹ חוֹ כָ חַ

.d אָ בְּ כֻ נֶ ע הֻ חֵי תֵי תוֹ חוֹ הוּ

Read aloud the following single-syllable combinations.

.e תַח אָח שַח נָח אַךְ בְּ לָךְ רַךְ

.f כֶּן כֶּם חֵית חֵיל חָל חוֹל כָּל כֹּה

The following reading practice focuses on distinguishing between look-alike letters. Read each single-syllable combination aloud.

.g תֵּה חֵת חַת חַר הַל הל חֵל תֵּל

.h כֵּר נֵר אֵין אֵיךְ עֵר עַר עַת אָח

.i מוֹךְ מוֹן מוֹר נוֹר כֵּר בֵּם כֶּם נֵם

Read aloud the following longer combinations of letters and vowels.

.j לֶכְנָה לָחֶם לָכֶן בְּכֶן בְּ לְכָה לֵךְ

.k נֵכָל נוֹכַח נָכָה נְכוֹת נָכֶה נֵכֵא

.l אָרוּךְ אָרְחֵי אָרַח אוֹרַךְ אוֹרֵךְ אוֹרֵן

.m רַחֵם רַכְרַךְ רָכְלָן רָכַן רָכַשׁ רְכָה

.n שׁוֹלַחַת שָׁלַח שָׁלְכֶן שֶׁלָּכֶם שֶׁלְּךָ שֶׁלָּךְ

.o חֶמְרַת חֲמָרָה חֲמוֹר חוֹמֶר חָמֵשׁ חָמֵשׁ

p. בֵּיתֵךְ בֵּיתְךָ בֵּיתֶךָ בֵּיתְכֶם בֵּיתְכֶן

q. עָכַר עַכְבָּר עַכְבָּרוֹן עַכְבְּרוֹשׁ עַכְבְּרָן

In this chapter, two new vowel symbols are introduced. One is written next to the Hebrew letter and the other is written beneath the Hebrew letter. Both indicate the same vowel sound.

sounds like **oo** as in f**oo**d	■וּ *(The ■ represents any Hebrew letter.)*
sounds like **oo** as in f**oo**d	■ֻ *(The ■ represents any Hebrew letter.)*

The וּ vowel looks very much like the וֹ vowel introduced in Chapter 2. The only difference in appearance between the two vowels is where the dot is placed.

You might remember this difference by picturing both vowels as human figures; a ball having been thrown into the stomach of the וּ vowel, it says "ooh!" while a bright idea has just occurred to the וֹ vowel and a lightbulb is shining at the top of its head as it says "oh!"

Reading Practice

Read aloud the following letter and vowel combinations.

a. מוּ בֻּ לֻ שׁוּ אוּ כוּ נֻ תֻ רוּ הוּ חֻ

b. לוּל לוּךְ נוּךְ נוּם חוּם שׁוּם בֻּל רֻל

c. עוּן נוּן תוּן תוּךְ בּוּךְ רוּךְ רֻשׁ מֻשׁ

d. רוּם אָרוּם אָרוֹן עָרוּר עָרוֹר

e. רְכוּשׁ רְכוּשָׁה רְכוּשָׁן רָכוּן רַחוּם

f. חֻמָּשׁ חֻמוֹר חָכוּר עָכוּר הֻכְעַר

You have now learned the letters and vowels that spell two other basic Jewish vocabulary words:

בָּרוּךְ גמש בְּרָכָה

Both of these words come from the root ב-ר-ך, which has the basic meaning of "bless." The word בְּרָכָה means "blessing" or "benediction." The word בָּרוּךְ means "blessed" and is familiar to many Jews as the first word of the traditional phrase that begins Hebrew blessings.

The blessing phrase and the Priestly Benediction

You can now read all the letters and all but one vowel in the traditional phrase that begins Hebrew blessings. Remember that the combination יְיָ is used as a substitution for the unpronounceable four-letter name of God, and that it is usually pronounced "Adonai."

בָּרוּךְ אַתָּה יְיָ אֱלֹהֵינוּ מֶלֶךְ הָעוֹלָם...

Blessed are You, Eternal our God, Sovereign of the universe …

You can also read almost all of the letters and vowels in the following biblical verse, which is part of the Priestly Benediction in Numbers 6 and is used by many Jewish parents to bless their children on Shabbat and festival evenings. Notice that both the new root ב-ר-ך and the root שׁ-מ-ר, which you learned in Chapter 3, appear in this verse.

יְבָרֶכְךָ יְיָ וְיִשְׁמְרֶךָ.

May God bless you and keep you. (Numbers 6:24)

Which Syllable Is Accented?

The word מֶלֶךְ, which appears in the Hebrew blessing phrase above, is pronounced with the accent on the first, not the last, syllable. Although most words in Sephardic Hebrew are stressed on the last syllable, words that end with the vowel pattern ◻ ◻ֶ ◻ (the ◻ represents any Hebrew letter) form a category that is an exception to this rule. Such words are stressed on the syllable with the first ◻ֶ vowel. Read the following examples aloud, remembering to place the stress on the syllable with the first ◻ֶ vowel.

a. לֶחֶם רֶחֶם רֶכֶל רֶכֶשׁ אוֹמֶרֶת נוֹתֶנֶת

b. נֶשֶׁר נֶשֶׁךְ בֶּרֶךְ תֶּלֶם שׁוֹמֶרֶת חוֹלֶמֶת

THE ROOT ב-ר-ך

Since the root ב-ר-ך has the basic meaning of "bless," there are many phrases and expressions in Jewish life that use words from this root. At the *brit milah*, the new baby boy is welcomed in Hebrew with the phrase בָּרוּךְ הַבָּא, which means "blessed is he who has come." The feminine equivalent of this phrase is בְּרוּכָה הַבָּאָה—"blessed is she who has come." The phrase is used in the plural at weddings to welcome the couple under the *chupah*. The root ב-ר-ך also appears in the first two words of the prayer said on behalf of those who are ill. This prayer, called the *Mi Shebeirach*, takes its name from these first two words: מִי שֶׁבֵּרַךְ, "May the One who blessed...." (The vowel that appears under and alongside the letter מ has not yet been introduced.)

The following are other Hebrew words formed from the root ב-ר-ך. This book has introduced most, but not all, of the letters and vowels appearing in these words. Remember that if a suffix is attached, and the final root letter ך is no longer the last letter of the word, it will appear as a regular כ.

Birkat HaMazon (Grace after Meals)	—	בִּרְכַּת הַמָּזוֹן
blessed	—	מְבֹרָךְ
knee	—	בֶּרֶךְ
to be blessed, to bless oneself	—	לְהִתְבָּרֵךְ
pond, pool	—	בְּרֵכָה
wild duck, mallard	—	בְּרֵכִיָּה

Excerpts

Following are prayer book excerpts that contain the root ב-ר-ךְ. You may already be familiar with the words or melodies of these prayers, though this book has not yet introduced some of the Hebrew letters and vowels that appear in them. Perhaps your teacher or a friend can read or sing these prayer book excerpts to you.

Try to find the root ב-ר-ךְ in each excerpt. (The number of occurrences of the root in each excerpt is indicated in parentheses.) In several cases, prefixes and suffixes are attached.

Bar'chu (4 occurrences)

בָּרְכוּ אֶת יְיָ הַמְבֹרָךְ.
בָּרוּךְ יְיָ הַמְבֹרָךְ לְעוֹלָם וָעֶד.

Third verse of *Shalom Aleichem* (2 occurrences)

בָּרְכוּנִי לְשָׁלוֹם, מַלְאֲכֵי הַשָּׁלוֹם, מַלְאֲכֵי עֶלְיוֹן, מִמֶּלֶךְ מַלְכֵי
הַמְּלָכִים, הַקָּדוֹשׁ בָּרוּךְ הוּא.

The end of *Birkat Shalom—Shalom Rav* and *Sim Shalom* (3 occurrences)

וְטוֹב בְּעֵינֶיךָ לְבָרֵךְ אֶת עַמְּךָ יִשְׂרָאֵל בְּכָל עֵת וּבְכָל שָׁעָה
בִּשְׁלוֹמֶךָ. בָּרוּךְ אַתָּה יְיָ, הַמְבָרֵךְ אֶת עַמּוֹ יִשְׂרָאֵל בַּשָּׁלוֹם.

The end of the blessing after the Haftarah reading (3 occurrences)

עַל הַכֹּל יְיָ אֱלֹהֵינוּ, אֲנַחְנוּ מוֹדִים לָךְ, וּמְבָרְכִים אוֹתָךְ, יִתְבָּרַךְ
שִׁמְךָ בְּפִי כָּל חַי תָּמִיד לְעוֹלָם וָעֶד. בָּרוּךְ אַתָּה יְיָ, מְקַדֵּשׁ הַשַּׁבָּת.

These are the block print forms of the Hebrew letters and one of the vowels introduced in this chapter. (The other vowel introduced in this chapter is simply written in both block print and script as three diagonal dots underneath the Hebrew letter.)

וּ וֹ דּ ךָ כּ חֵ ח

These are their script forms.

וּ וֹ קּ ךַ כּ חֵ ח

Hebrew Writing Exercises

1. Write a line of the letter *Chet*, using either block print or script.

_____ ח

2. Write a line of the letter *Kaf*, using either block print or script.

_____ כ

3. Write a line of the letter *Kaf Sofit* (Final *Kaf*), using either block print or script.

_____ ך

4. Write a line of the new vowel, using either block print or script.

_____ וֹ

Exercises

1. Draw a line connecting each Hebrew consonant and vowel combination with the English word that has the same sound.

tube	נוּן	loom		בּוּן
sure	מוּת	shoot		רֻל
noon	שֻׁר	rule		לוֹם
moot	תֻּב	boon		שֻׁת

2. Write the Hebrew consonant and vowel combinations that sound like the following English words. There is more than one possibility for each word.

   a. toot _____   **b.** loot _____   **c.** lure _____

   _____   _____   _____

   d. tour _____   **e.** boor _____   **f.** boom _____

   _____   _____   _____

   g. room _____   **h.** tomb _____   **i.** tune _____

   _____   _____   _____

   j. moon _____   **k.** hoot _____   **l.** newt _____

   _____   _____   _____

3. Following are Hebrew names that you may know. Read each word aloud and connect it to its English equivalent below.

Ruth	רָחֵל	Nachshon	בְּרָכָה
Nachman	רוּת	Chanan	נַחוּם
Rachel	מְנַחֵם	Nachum	חָנָן
Baruch	נֶחָמָה	Chana (Hannah)	נָחוֹר
Nechamah	בָּרוּךְ	Nachor	חַנָּה
Menachem	נַחְמָן	Bracha	נַחְשׁוֹן

4. The following reading practice focuses on look-alike letters that can be easily confused. Read each combination aloud.

a. חוֹם חוֹם תוֹם תוּם תוּת חוּת הוּר

b. חָנָה חָכָה חָכָן חָנָן תָּנָן תָּנֵךְ תָּנַח

c. נוּר נוֹר כוֹר בּוּר בּוֹר בּוּל כּוּל

d. עוֹנָה עוֹנַת אָנָה אָנַח אָנַת אַחַת

e. בְּרִי כְּרִי נְרִי נְתִי כְּתִי נְחִי כְּנִי

5. Read aloud the following letter and vowel combinations.

אָח   אַחַר   אַחֲרֵי   אַחֵר   אַחֶרֶת   אַחֲרֹן   .a

בָּחַן   בֹּחַן   בּוֹשֶׁן   בָּחַר   בָּחַשׁ   בְּחוּשׁ   .b

לֵךְ   לַח   לֵחָה   לַחוּת   לְחַךְ   לְכָלֵךְ   .c

מָלֵא   מְלוֹא   מִלְאוּ   מְלֵאת   מְמֻלָּא   .d

לֶחֶם   תֶּרֶם   חֶרֶם   לֶמֶךְ   לְחֶךְ   עֶרֶךְ   .e

חָשַׁשׁ   חָשַׁךְ   חָשׁוּךְ   חֲשָׁשָׁה   חֲשֵׁכָה   .f

נַחַל   נָחָר   נָחוֹר   נְחוּר   נֵכָר   נֵחָן   .g

חָתָה   חָתָן   חָתַם   חָתוּם   חָתַךְ   חָתוּךְ   .h

רַחוּם   מְרַחֵם   מְרֻחֶמֶת   תְּרַחֵם   נְרַחֵם   .i

חִכָּה   חָכָם   חַכְמָן   חָתַר   חָתוּל   .j

לוֹחֵשׁ   לוֹחֶשֶׁת   לְחֶשֶׁת   לַחְשָׁן   לַחַשׁ   .k

אַשּׁוּר   אֲשֶׁר   אֲשֵׁרָה   אִשַּׁרְנוּ   מְאֻשָּׁר   .l

עֶרֶךְ   עוֹרֵךְ   עֶרְכֵי   עָרַכְתָּ   עֲרַכְתְּ   .m

מֶלֶךְ   מֶלַח   מַלְאַךְ   מְלָחָה   מְלֵחוּת   .n

לָחַךְ   לָחֶם   מַלְחֵם   מְלַחֵךְ   לְכָלְכֶן   .o

רְכַן   רָכוּן   הֻרְכַּן   הֻרְכֵּן   הַרְכְּנָה   .p

עָרוּךְ   אָרוּם   אָרוּר   אָחוּר   רְכוּשׁ   .q

6. Read aloud the following words taken from the prayer book.

בָּרְכוּ   רָאוּ   עָנוּ   אָמְרוּ   שָׁמְרוּ   הוּא   .a

לְכָה   לְכוּ   נֵלְכָה   לָכֶם   כַּלָּה   כָּלוּ   .b

חֵן   חַנּוּן   רַחוּם   רַחֵם   הַמְרַחֵם   .c

עָלֵינוּ   מֵעָלֵינוּ   עֵינֵינוּ   שׁוֹמְרֵנוּ   מְנוּחָתֵנוּ   לֵאלֹהֵינוּ   .d
לֵאלֹהֵיכֶם

מַלְכֵי   מַלְכוּתוֹ   מַלְכוּתֶךָ   מֶמְשַׁלְתֶּךָ   מְלַאכְתּוֹ   מַלְכוּתָהּ   .e
תִּשְׁבְּחָתָא

EXTRA CREDIT
The Letter כ Used as Prefix and Suffix

The letter כ often is used as a prefix and its final form ך is used as a suffix.

When the final letter ך is attached to the end of a word, it is generally translated as either "you" or "your." It usually appears with one of two vowels, either as ךָ or as ךְ.

Following are some examples:

your peace	—	שְׁלוֹמֶךְ	peace	—	שָׁלוֹם
your name	—	שְׁמֶךְ	name	—	שֵׁם
your Torah	—	תּוֹרָתֶךְ	Torah	—	תּוֹרָה
when you are walking	—	בְּלֶכְתְּךְ	when walking	—	בְּלֶכֶת

When the letter כ is attached to the beginning of a word, it is equivalent to the English preposition "as" or "like." An example of this is found in the first two verses of the well-known hymn *Ein Keloheinu*. The letter כ appears with a dot in the first verse and without a dot in the second verse for grammatical reasons that do not affect the meaning of the prefix.

אֵין כֵּאלֹהֵינוּ, אֵין כַּאדוֹנֵינוּ, אֵין כְּמַלְכֵּנוּ, אֵין כְּמוֹשִׁיעֵנוּ.
מִי כֵאלֹהֵינוּ, מִי כַאדוֹנֵינוּ, מִי כְמַלְכֵּנוּ, מִי כְמוֹשִׁיעֵנוּ?

There is none **like** our God; there is none **like** our Ruler, there is none **like** our Sovereign, there is none **like** our Redeemer.

Who is **like** our God; who is **like** our Ruler; who is **like** our Sovereign; who is **like** our Redeemer?

Review

You have now learned the following Hebrew letters.

שׁ בּ תּ ל מ ם ס ה ר א

עַ נ ן כ ח ך

You have learned ten vowel symbols.

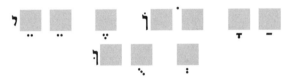

And you have learned seven basic Jewish vocabulary words.

שַׁבָּת שָׁלוֹם תּוֹרָה שֵׁם שְׁמַע

בָּרוּךְ בְּרָכָה

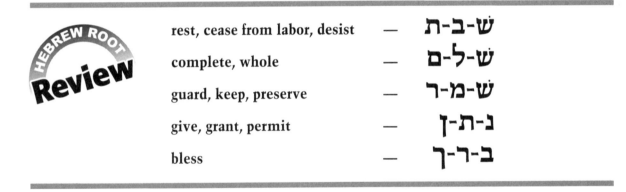

rest, cease from labor, desist	—	שׁ-ב-ת
complete, whole	—	שׁ-ל-ם
guard, keep, preserve	—	שׁ-מ-ר
give, grant, permit	—	נ-ת-ן
bless	—	ב-ר-ך

This chapter introduces two letters with the same sound: *Bet* (without the dot in the center) and *Vav*. In Chapter 1, we introduced the sound of the letter *Bet* written with a dot in the middle, which is the same as the sound of the English letter *b*. In this chapter, the sound of the letter *Bet* without the dot is introduced.

Bet (without a dot)	**v** as in **v**est	ב
Vav	**v** as in **v**est	ו

Vav—Vowel and Consonant

The letter *Vav* can act both as a vowel and as a consonant in Hebrew. You have already learned the two vowel sounds that can be represented by using the letter *Vav* with a dot above or in the center of the letter:

וֹ וּ

When the letter *Vav* acts as a consonant, it generally appears without a dot. And unless it is the last letter of a word, the consonant *Vav* is written with an accompanying vowel. Read aloud the following examples.

וַי וֶל וּול וָל וָו מָו שָׁו מוּ מוֹ מֶו

Look-Alike Letters

The letter *Bet* and the letter *Kaf* that you learned in the last chapter look very much alike. Notice that the *Kaf* has a curved shape, while the *Bet* has a bottom bar that extends beyond the back of the letter.

בּ כ

The letters *Vav* and *Nun Sofit* (Final *Nun*) also look very much alike. The *Vav*, however, is shorter than the *Nun Sofit*, which drops down below the line of print. And the letter *Vav* can appear in any position within a word, while the *Nun Sofit* can appear only as the last letter.

ו ן

Reading Practice

Say aloud the sound of the following letters, which include those from previous chapters as well as the new letters. Say the word "silent" for those letters that are silent. Try to do this without looking at the chart on the previous page.

a. בּ ב ו ז ן ן נ ב כ ר ת ח ת ה

b. מ ו ן ע ל כ ב ס ו שׁ ו א ב

Read aloud the following letter and vowel combinations.

c. בָּ וְ ן בֵּי וֶ בַּ וָ ב וּו בוּ וְ בְּ

d. בְ בַּ כָ נְ וּו וו הוֹ חוֹ תוּ בוֹ בֵ

Read aloud the following single-syllable combinations.

e. תֹּב לֵב הֹב חָו כָו כֻו בֻו בָם בָן בָךְ

f. לֵב שֵׁב נֵיב רֵיב בֵּב מֵבְ מְבְ עְב

g. תָו הֻו שׁוּ אֹו אֹון וֹון וֹום בֹּו בּוּךְ

The following reading practice focuses on distinguishing between look-alike letters. Read each combination aloud.

h. זָן נָזָן כַּזָן כַּוָנָה כַּנֶּה כַּנּוּ כָּנוּ בָּנוּ

i. חֵן הֵן הֵו חֹון חֹוךְ חָוְךְ חָנָךְ חַבָּךְ

j. תּוֹבָה חוֹבַת חוֹבָה תוֹכָה תֹונָה חַוָה

Read aloud the following combinations of letters and vowels.

k. שָׁוֶה שָׁוָה נָוֶה נָוָה שָׁלֵו שָׁלוּ שַׁלְוָה

l. רֹוב מֶרֹב בָּרֹב רְחֹוב הַתֹוב הַתֵב

m. לֵבֶן אֶבֶן אָבַּר שֶׁבֶר וְשֶׁת וְשֶׁךְ

n. בְּנֵי בְּעֵי בְּעֹון בְּנֹון נְבֹון נְבֹוךְ נְבֹום

o. עֶרֶב חֶרֶב חָרָב כְּרוּב כְּרָבָה כְּרָב

p. וְתֶר וָתָר וַתְּרָן וַתְּרָה וַתְּרַת וַתְרָנוּת

You have now learned the letters and vowels that spell another basic Jewish vocabulary word:

תְּשׁוּבָה

This word is most often translated as "repentance," although that translation does not fully convey the meaning of the Hebrew. The word comes from the root שׁ-ו-ב, which has the basic meaning of "return" or "come back." One who does *t'shuvah* is one who, after going astray, returns or comes back to the right path.

Deuteronomy Rabbah 2:12

You can now read almost every Hebrew letter in the following quote. This quote, taken from the rabbinic literature, appears on the frontispiece of the High Holy Day prayer book *Gates of Repentance*.

שַׁעֲרֵי תְשׁוּבָה לְעוֹלָם פְּתוּחִין.

The gates of repentance are always open.

Vav as a Prefix

The letter *Vav* often appears as a prefix attached to the beginning of a Hebrew word. This prefix can have different meanings, but a common meaning is the word "and." Usually when the letter *Vav* appears as a prefix, it will be a consonant with a vowel written under it.

וְשַׁבָּת   וְשָׁלוֹם   וְשָׁמְרוּ   וֵאלֹהֵי   וְשֵׁם

In certain instances, however, the prefix *Vav* will appear as the vowel וּ. In such cases, the word begins with a vowel that is not preceded by a consonant. Read aloud the examples below.

וּבֵין   וּבָרוּךְ   וּבְרָכָה   וּמֹשֶׁה   וּכְתַבְתָּם

In this chapter, four new vowel symbols are introduced. Two of them represent sounds that are identical to other vowels you have already learned. The other two symbols represent one new vowel sound that can be written in two ways, either as a single symbol beneath the Hebrew letter or as symbols written both beneath and to the left of the Hebrew letter.

sounds like **ah** as in father	▨ᵥ (The ▨ represents any Hebrew letter.)
sounds like **eh** as in bed	▨ (The ▨ represents any Hebrew letter.)
sounds like **ee** as in feet	▨ (The ▨ represents any Hebrew letter.)
sounds like **ee** as in feet	▨י (The ▨ represents any Hebrew letter.)

Note: *Within the system of Sephardic Hebrew, there are some variations in pronunciation. One of these variations concerns the pronunciation of the vowel ▨. In America, most treat the vowel ▨ as identical in sound to the vowel יִ, just as is indicated in the chart above. In Israel, however, the vowel ▨ is often pronounced as a shorter vowel sound than the vowel יִ, like the short i sound in* fit *instead of the long* ee *sound in* feet.

The Vowels ▨ and ▨

The vowels ▨ and ▨ are almost identical in sound to the vowels ▨ and ▨ respectively. They are formed by combining the ▨ and ▨ vowels with the ▨ vowel. You will see these combination vowels used under the silent letters א and ע, the gutteral letter ח, and the letter ה.

Reading Practice

Read aloud the following letter and vowel combinations.

.a   הִיא   תִי   בִי   נִי   וִי   כִי   בִי   רִי   מִי   לִי   בִּי

.b   רִיךְ   לִיךְ   כִים   לִים   עִים   חִין   תִין   שִין

.c   הֲכִי   עֲמְ   אֲנִי   וְאִי   וְנִי   שְׁבִי   בְּלִי   תְּרִי

.d   לוֹ   רוֹ   כוֹ   כְּב   תְּב   נְב   נְשׁ   לְשׁ   בְּשׁ

.e   חֲלוֹם   אַלְמָה   חָתוּךְ   חֲנוֹךְ   אֱמֹר   חֲמוֹר

.f   אֱמוּנַת   אֱמוּנָה   אֱמוֹן   אֱמוּל   אֱלוּל   אֱלִי

.g   אַהֲבָה   תְּאַהֲבִי   אֱהֲבִי   לֶאֱהֹב   אֱהַב

The last word you read on the line above is another basic Hebrew vocabulary word:

אַהֲבָה

This is a noun meaning "love." Many prayers and biblical passages speak of God's love for us and our obligation to love one another.

The word אַהֲבָה comes from the root א-ה-ב, which has the basic meaning of "love" or "affection." The root א-ה-ב appears in the well-known biblical quote: וְאָהַבְתָּ לְרֵעֲךָ כָּמוֹךָ—"You shall love your neighbor as yourself (Leviticus 19:18)."

The following are other Hebrew words formed from the root א-ה-ב. You can now read all the letters and vowels that appear in these words.

lover	—	אוֹהֵב
sweetheart, beloved	—	אָהוּב
suitor, lover	—	מְאַהֵב
flirtation	—	אַהֲבְהָבִים
philanderer	—	אַהֲבָן
enamored, lovesick	—	מְאֹהָב

PRAYER BOOK Excerpts The following are prayer book excerpts that contain words from the root א-ה-ב. You may already be familiar with the words or melodies of these prayers, though this book has not yet introduced some of the Hebrew letters and vowels appearing in them. Perhaps your teacher or a friend can read or sing these prayer book excerpts to you.

Try to find the root א-ה-ב in each excerpt. (The number of occurrences of the root in each excerpt is indicated in parentheses.) In most cases, prefixes and suffixes are attached. And in one case, the vowel וֹ appears between two root letters.

V'ahavta (Deut. 6:5) (1 occurrence)

וְאָהַבְתָּ אֵת יְהוָה אֱלֹהֶיךָ, בְּכָל לְבָבְךָ, וּבְכָל נַפְשְׁךָ, וּבְכָל מְאֹדֶךָ.

Shabbat evening *Kiddush* (2 occurrences)

בָּרוּךְ אַתָּה יְיָ אֱלֹהֵינוּ מֶלֶךְ הָעוֹלָם, אֲשֶׁר קִדְּשָׁנוּ בְּמִצְוֹתָיו
וְרָצָה בָנוּ, וְשַׁבַּת קָדְשׁוֹ בְּאַהֲבָה וּבְרָצוֹן הִנְחִילָנוּ, זִכָּרוֹן
לְמַעֲשֵׂה בְרֵאשִׁית. כִּי הוּא יוֹם תְּחִלָּה לְמִקְרָאֵי קֹדֶשׁ, זֵכֶר
לִיצִיאַת מִצְרָיִם. כִּי בָנוּ בָחַרְתָּ וְאוֹתָנוּ קִדַּשְׁתָּ מִכָּל הָעַמִּים,
וְשַׁבַּת קָדְשְׁךָ בְּאַהֲבָה וּבְרָצוֹן הִנְחַלְתָּנוּ. בָּרוּךְ אַתָּה יְיָ,
מְקַדֵּשׁ הַשַּׁבָּת.

Ahavat Olam (4 occurrences)

אַהֲבַת עוֹלָם בֵּית יִשְׂרָאֵל עַמְּךָ אָהָבְתָּ...
וְאַהֲבָתְךָ אַל תָּסִיר מִמֶּנּוּ לְעוֹלָמִים. בָּרוּךְ אַתָּה יְיָ,
אוֹהֵב עַמּוֹ יִשְׂרָאֵל.

Ahavah Rabbah (5 occurrences)

אַהֲבָה רַבָּה אֲהַבְתָּנוּ, יְיָ אֱלֹהֵינוּ...
וְהָאֵר עֵינֵינוּ בְּתוֹרָתֶךָ, וְדַבֵּק לִבֵּנוּ בְּמִצְוֹתֶיךָ, וְיַחֵד לְבָבֵנוּ
לְאַהֲבָה וּלְיִרְאָה אֶת שְׁמֶךָ...
וּבָנוּ בָחַרְתָּ וְקֵרַבְתָּנוּ לְשִׁמְךָ הַגָּדוֹל סֶלָה בֶּאֱמֶת לְהוֹדוֹת לְךָ
וּלְיַחֶדְךָ בְּאַהֲבָה. בָּרוּךְ אַתָּה יְיָ, הַבּוֹחֵר בְּעַמּוֹ יִשְׂרָאֵל
בְּאַהֲבָה.

These are the block print forms of the Hebrew letters introduced in this chapter.

ב בּ ו וּ

These are their script forms.

ב אּ ו וּ

Hebrew Writing Exercises

1. Write a line of the letter *Bet* (without the dot), using either block print or script.

_____ ב

2. Write a line of the letter *Vav*, using either block print or script.

_____ ו

Exercises

1. Draw a line connecting each Hebrew consonant and vowel combination with the English word that has the same sound.

behave	נֵל	shave	רוֹב
knave	מֵב	vote	וֵין
move	נוּ	vein	שֵׁב
kneel	בְּהֵיב	rove	ווֹת

2. Write the Hebrew consonant and vowel combinations that sound like the following English words. There is more than one possibility for each word.

a. sheet _____   **b.** shear _____   **c.** here _____

_____   _____   _____

d. near _____   **e.** ear _____   **f.** eel _____

_____   _____   _____

g. veal _____   **h.** heave _____   **i.** leave _____

_____   _____   _____

j. mean _____   **k.** bean _____   **l.** beam _____

_____   _____   _____

3. The following reading practice focuses on look-alike letters that can be easily confused. Read each combination aloud.

a. בִּיש בִיש כְש נְש וִיש וָש וָן נָן

b. עָוָן עָנָן עָכָן עָבָן עָבָו עָכוּ עָנוּ

c. תֵבָה חֵבָה הֵבָה הֵכָה תֵכָה כוּ כֵן

d. בְּרִי בְּכֵי בְּכִי בְּנֵי בְּוִי בְּתֵי בְּחֵי

e. תּוֹם חוּם חוֹם הוֹם הוּם תוֹם תָּוֶם

f. אָכַל אָבַל אָנַל אֶנַן אָווֹן אָנוֹךְ

g. אָבִיו אָנִיו אָכִיו אָכִין אָבִין אָבִיךְ

h. וְהֵל וַחֵל וָתֵל וַבֵּל וָכֵל וְבֵל וַנֵל

i. בִּימֵה בְמֵה כְמֵה נְמֵה וּמֵה וִימֵה

Many Hebrew words are part of the vocabulary of those who live a Jewish life. Hebrew names and words for ritual objects, holiday, and traditional practices are often familiar even to those who think they know no Hebrew. Starting with this chapter, every chapter will include a list of such words. Try to read the Hebrew first and see if you recognize the word before looking at the English translation.

Tel Aviv (*literally* "hill of spring")	—	תֵּל אָבִיב
Abraham	—	אַבְרָהָם
Aaron	—	אַהֲרֹן
palm branch	—	לוּלָב
Shavuot (*literally:* "weeks")	—	שָׁבוּעוֹת
Jewish law	—	הֲלָכָה
Mishnah	—	מִשְׁנָה
shivah (*literally:* "seven," for shivah is traditionally observed for seven days)	—	שִׁבְעָה
Shabbat Shuvah ("the Sabbath of Return"—the Shabbat that falls between Rosh HaShanah and Yom Kippur)	—	שַׁבָּת שׁוּבָה
the covenant of circumcision	—	בְּרִית מִילָה

CHAPTER 6

4. Read aloud the following letter and vowel combinations.

וּמִי　וּמִין　וּמֵי　וּבֵי　וּבֵין　וּבְנֵי　וּרְאֵה .a

וַאֲנִי　וַאֲרִי　וַאֵלִי　וֶאֱמֶת　וְאֶרֶת　וְאֵלִי .b

חֲבִי　חֲרִי　חֲרֵי　עֲרֵי　עֲמָמִי　עֲנֵי　עֲנִי .c

תַּאֲוָה　אַהֲבָה　תַּאֲוַת　תַּאֲוָן　תַּאֲווֹת .d

מְעֲנָה　מְעֲלֶה　מְעֲבָה　מְעֲבֶּרֶת　מְעֲנָן .e

נֶאֱלָם　נֶאֱמָן　נֶאֱהַב　נֶאֱכָל　נֶאֱנַשׁ .f

מַעֲבָר　מַעֲלָל　מַעֲנֶה　מַעֲרָב　מַעֲרָךְ .g

חֲבוּר　חֲבוּרָה　חֲבוּלָה　חֲבָלִים　חֲבוּלִי .h

בּוֹכֶה　בּוֹכִים　הוֹכִים　הוֹבִיל　הוֹאִיל .i

5. Read aloud the following words and phrases taken from the prayer book.

The *Bar'chu*

בָּרְכוּ אֶת יְיָ הַמְבֹרָךְ. .a

The ending of *Ma'ariv Aravim*

בָּרוּךְ אַתָּה יְיָ, הַמַּעֲרִיב עֲרָבִים. .b

Blessing over Havdalah candle

בָּרוּךְ אַתָּה יְיָ אֱלֹהֵינוּ מֶלֶךְ הָעוֹלָם, בּוֹרֵא מְאוֹרֵי הָאֵשׁ. .c

From the blessing before the Torah reading

אֲשֶׁר בָּחַר בָּנוּ ... וְנָתַן לָנוּ אֶת תּוֹרָתוֹ .d

From the Sabbath Psalm (Psalm 92)

שִׁיר לְיוֹם הַשַּׁבָּת ... לְשִׁמְךָ עֶלְיוֹן .e

From the *V'ahavta*

בְּשִׁבְתְּךָ בְּבֵיתֶךָ וּבְלֶכְתְּךָ ... וּכְתַבְתָּם .f

From the *Kaddish*

בִּרְכָתָא וְשִׁירָתָא תֻּשְׁבְּחָתָא וְנֶחֱמָתָא .g

From the *Kaddish*

בְּרִיךְ הוּא ... וְאִמְרוּ אָמֵן .h

In many prayer books, the *V'ahavta* paragraph following the *Shema* looks like this:

וְאָהַבְתָּ אֵת יְהוָה אֱלֹהֶיךָ בְּכָל־לְבָבְךָ וּבְכָל־נַפְשְׁךָ וּבְכָל־מְאֹדֶךָ:
וְהָיוּ הַדְּבָרִים הָאֵלֶּה אֲשֶׁר אָנֹכִי מְצַוְּךָ הַיּוֹם עַל־לְבָבֶךָ:
וְשִׁנַּנְתָּם לְבָנֶיךָ וְדִבַּרְתָּ בָּם בְּשִׁבְתְּךָ בְּבֵיתֶךָ וּבְלֶכְתְּךָ בַדֶּרֶךְ
וּבְשָׁכְבְּךָ וּבְקוּמֶךָ: וּקְשַׁרְתָּם לְאוֹת עַל־יָדֶךָ וְהָיוּ לְטֹטָפֹת בֵּין
עֵינֶיךָ: וּכְתַבְתָּם עַל־מְזוּזֹת בֵּיתֶךָ וּבִשְׁעָרֶיךָ:

If you look closely at this text, you can see that in addition to the Hebrew vowel symbols that you have learned, there are other dots and marks written above and below the Hebrew letters. For example, in the word וְאָהַבְתָּ, there are two dots above the תָּ and a right-angle shaped mark next to the vowel under the א. These marks are called *trope* or *cantillation* marks.

All the books of the Bible have trope marks accompanying the Hebrew text. These trope marks serve three purposes. They act as an aid to pronunciation, for the trope marks are always written above or below the syllables that are accented in each word. They form a system of punctuation, dividing paragraphs into verses and each verse into smaller units, as do periods, commas, and semicolons in English punctuation. And they indicate the system of chanting to be used in public recitations of the text, for each trope mark is associated with different musical phrases.

The trope system was developed sometime during the seventh or eighth century C.E. in order to insure a uniform reading and understanding of biblical texts. To appreciate the necessity for such a system, consider the appearance of the Hebrew writing in a Torah scroll.

ואהבת את יהוה אלהיך בכל לבבך ובכל נפשך
ובכל מאדך והיו הדברים האלה אשר אנכי מצוך
היום על לבבך ושננתם לבניך ודברת בם בשבתך
בביתך ובלכתך בדרך ובשכבך ובקומך וקשרתם
לאות על ידך והיו לטטפת בין עיניך וכתבתם על
מזוזת ביתך ובשעריך

Torah scrolls are written the way that Hebrew was written in antiquity, without any vowels or punctuation. There is no indication of where each sentence or verse should begin or end. Without a standardized system, different readers could read and understand the same Torah passage differently.

The *V'ahavta* paragraph above is an excerpt from the Bible, from Deuteronomy 6:5–9. When it is chanted during a synagogue service, many congregations use the melody of the biblical trope. That is why this passage appears in many prayer books with the accompanying trope marks.

Review

You have now learned the following Hebrew letters.

ש ב ת ל מ ם ס ה ר א

ע נ ן ח ז כ ך ו ב

You have learned fourteen vowel symbols.

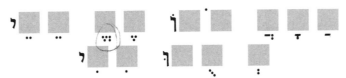

And you have learned nine basic Jewish vocabulary words.

שַׁבָּת שָׁלוֹם תּוֹרָה שֵׁם שְׁמַע

בָּרוּךְ בְּרָכָה תְּשׁוּבָה אַהֲבָה

(handwritten annotations: Hear, Name, Blessed, Love, Coming back to truth/Answer)

rest, cease from labor, desist	— ש-ב-ת
complete, whole	— ש-ל-ם
guard, keep, preserve	— ש-מ-ר
give, grant, permit	— נ-ת-ן
bless	— ב-ר-ך
love, affection	— א-ה-ב

This chapter introduces three new letters. One of them, the letter *Tzadi*, represents a sound that is found in English only in the middle or at the end of a word. The letter *Tzadi* is one of the five Hebrew letters that have both a regular form and a final form.

Tzadi	**ts** as in ca**ts**	צ
Tzadi Sofit (Final *Tzadi*)	**ts** as in ca**ts**	ץ
Dalet	**d** as in **d**oor	ד
Yod	**y** as in **y**ellow	י

Yod—Vowel and Consonant

The letter *Yod*, like the letter *Vav* discussed in the last chapter, can act both as a vowel and consonant in Hebrew. You have already learned two vowel symbols that utilize the letter *Yod* together with dots under the preceding Hebrew letter: יָ יִ

When the letter *Yod* acts as a vowel, it is written without another vowel symbol under or following it. When it acts as a consonant, it generally appears with an accompanying vowel. Read aloud the following examples.

אִיר אָיר אִיל אֵיל יֵל יוּ יוֹ יְה יֶה יָה

Look-Alike Letters

The letters *Dalet* and *Reish* look very much alike. Notice that the letter *Reish*, which sounds like *r*, has a **r**ounded back, while the letter *Dalet* has a top bar that extends beyond the back of the letter.

ד ר

The two letters *Dalet* and *Kaf Sofit* (Final *Kaf*) also look very much alike. The *Dalet*, however, is shorter than the *Kaf Sofit*, which drops down below the line of print. And the letter *Dalet* can appear in any position within a word, while the *Kaf Sofit* can appear only as the last letter.

ד ך

Some Hebrew learners confuse the *Tzadi* and the *Aleph* because they have similar shapes. They can be distinguished by noting that a horizontal bar forms the bottom of the *Tzadi*.

צ א

In some Hebrew print styles, the letters *Tzadi* and *Ayin* both have a horizontal bar across the bottom of the letter. In the style used in this book, the bar across the bottom of the letter *Ayin* curves up to the right, making it less likely to be confused with the letter *Tzadi*. The two letters can also be distinguished by the short upper right arm, attached to the middle of the center diagonal bar in the letter *Tzadi*.

ע　צ

Reading Practice

Say aloud the sounds of the following letters, which include those from previous chapters as well as the new letters. Say the word "silent" for those letters that are silent. Try to do this without looking at the chart on the previous page.

.a　ד　ר　ד　ר　ד　ד　י　ו　י　צ　י　א　צ　ע

.b　י　ו　ז　ן　צ　ץ　ע　צ　ע　צ　י　ו　נ　כ　ב　ב

.c　צ　א　צ　ץ　ז　ן　ד　ר　ד　ח　ה　ה　ת

Read aloud the following letter and vowel combinations.

.d　דָ　דְ　דֶ　דֵ　דִ　דֹי　יֹו　יֻ　יִ　צֵ　צֵי　צַ　צֻו

.e　אָ　צַ　עַ　דֵי　רֵי　דִי　יִי　יֵי　יָ　יִ　צָ　צֻו

.f　צֵ　דַ　דִי　יִי　יֹו　צַ　צֵי　דֵ　דֹו　צַ　צֶ　יֹ

Read aloud the following single-syllable combinations.

.g　רֵץ　מָץ　שָׁץ　עֵץ　לֵץ　יֵץ　נָץ　בָּץ　חָץ

.h　וָד　נַד　כַד　בַד　בַד　בָּד　בַּר　בֶּךְ　בֶּן

.i　צֹום　צָאן　יֹון　יֹון　צֹון　אֹון　צִיר　צַיד

.j　דִים　דָם　דַם　דֵךְ　רֵךְ　יֵךְ　יַךְ　יָץ　יֵץ

Read aloud the following longer combinations of letters and vowels.

.k　צָמָה　צָרָה　צָדָה　צִוָה　צָנָה　צָלָה　צָבָא

.l　שֶׁרֶץ　אֶרֶץ　מֶרֶץ　תֶּרֶץ　בֶּרֶץ　לֶרֶץ　נֶרֶץ

.m　יָדַע　יָרַע　יֵשֵׁב　יָרַד　תָּרַד　נֵרַד　אָרַד

n. יָרָם הִירָם יִירָא בִּירָה וַיִּרַע יָרַע

o. עֲמֹד תַּעֲמֹד עָבֹד תַּעֲבֹד לַעֲבֹד עָבְדִּי

p. דְּלוּל דְּלַל דְּלָלָה דִּלְלוּ דִּלֵּל דִּלְלָה

q. אֶחָד אָחָד לְאֶחָד נֶאֱחָד יֵאָחֵד

r. צָרוּב צוֹרֵב צָרֹב צָרִיךְ צָרְכָן צְרִיכָה

You have now learned the letters and vowels that spell another Jewish vocabulary word:

מִצְוָה

This word comes from the Hebrew root צ-ו-ה, whose basic meaning is "command." The word *mitzvah* literally means "a commandment," although it is often used colloquially to mean "a good deed." According to tradition, there are 613 commandments in the Torah. Since many of them concern ethical acts that are good deeds, it is not surprising that the word has come to be used with this meaning.

The plural of the word *mitzvah* is *mitzvot*: מִצְוֹת.

The appearance of this word can be confusing, because the letter *Vav* looks like it is the *oh* vowel accompanying the consonant צ. In fact, the consonant צ already has a vowel, the ְ vowel, and the letter *Vav* is a consonant *v* with the *oh* sound indicated by the vowel dot above.

The blessing phrase

In Chapter 5, we examined the traditional phrase that begins Hebrew blessings. When the blessing concerns the performance of a mitzvah, the opening phrase is longer, with an additional clause added. This clause includes the plural word מִצְוֹת, with a prefix and a suffix attached.

You can now read all but one letter in the following phrase. The last word contains one unusual letter *Vav*, which acts as a consonant while having a dot in the middle.

בָּרוּךְ אַתָּה יְיָ אֱלֹהֵינוּ מֶלֶךְ הָעוֹלָם, אֲשֶׁר קִדְּשָׁנוּ בְּמִצְוֹתָיו, וְצִוָּנוּ...

Blessed are You, Eternal our God, Sovereign of the universe, who makes us holy with mitzvot and commands us …

Accent Marks

The blessing phrase above is printed as it appears in most prayer books. If you look closely at the words אֱלֹהֵינוּ, מֶלֶךְ, קִדְּשָׁנוּ, and וְצִוָּנוּ, you will notice that they each have a small vertical line written next to one of the vowels underneath the word. This line functions as an accent mark and indicates the syllable that is stressed in pronouncing the word. As a general rule, words that do not have such a mark are stressed on the last syllable. From now on, all the prayer book excerpts in this book will include these accent marks.

In this chapter, we introduce one new vowel sound, which is formed using symbols you have already learned.

BUY. BU+Y.

sounds like **ie** as in p**ie** or **y** as in sk**y**	יִ *(The ⬜ represents any Hebrew letter.)*

Reading Practice

Read aloud the following letter and vowel combinations.

a. חַי לַי תַי דַי אַי מַי בַּי צַי רַי נַי

b. שַׁדַּי יָדַי אַחַי בָּנַי הָרַי חַיֵּי עֲבָדַי

c. דַּיָּנֵי יְלָדַי צְלָעַי צְרָכַי דְּרָכַי דַּיֵּנוּ

d. אֲבוֹתַי אִמּוֹתַי אֱלֹהַי אֱלֹהֶיךָ חַיִּים

The last word you read on the line above is another basic Hebrew vocabulary word: חַיִּים. This is a noun meaning "life." It is also used as a man's name. And, with the prefix לְ, it is a widely known Hebrew salutation meaning "to life!": לְחַיִּים.

The Letter *Yod* with Other Vowels

Occasionally, you will see an unvoweled letter *Yod* following the [ ] vowel or the [ ] vowel. In such cases, the letter *Yod* is silent and does not affect the pronunciation of the preceding vowel. Read aloud the following examples:

בְּמִצְוֹתָיו מִצְוֹתֶיךָ עֵינֶיךָ וּבִשְׁעָרֶיךָ

When, however, the unvoweled letter *Yod* follows the [ ] vowel *at the end of a word*, it sounds exactly the same as the combination יַ [ ]. Perhaps the best-known example of such an occurrence is the word: אֲדֹנָי. Another well-known example is the word: מִצְוֹתָי.

THE ROOT צ-ו-ה

The word מִצְוָה comes from the root צ-ו-ה, which has the basic meaning of "command" or "order."

The following are examples of Hebrew words formed from the root צ-ו-ה. When the letter ה is the last letter of a root, it sometimes does not appear in words formed from that root. In one of the examples below, the letter ה has dropped out and only the root letters ו and צ remain.

commands, commander, governor	— מְצַוֶּה
bound to, obliged to, ordered	— מְצֻוֶּה
he commanded	— צִוָּה
command, order, imperative	— צִוּוּי

Try to find the root ה-ו-צ in each of the following prayer book excerpts. The number of occurrences of the root in each excerpt is indicated in parentheses. In every case but one, the letter ה has dropped out and only the root letters ו and צ remain. There are also prefixes and suffixes attached.

The opening phrase for Hebrew blessings (2 occurrences)

בָּרוּךְ אַתָּה יְיָ אֱלֹהֵינוּ מֶלֶךְ הָעוֹלָם, אֲשֶׁר קִדְּשָׁנוּ בְּמִצְוֹתָיו וְצִוָּנוּ

From the *V'ahavta* (Deut. 6:5–6) (1 occurrence)

וְאָהַבְתָּ אֵת יְהוָה אֱלֹהֶיךָ בְּכָל לְבָבְךָ וּבְכָל נַפְשְׁךָ וּבְכָל מְאֹדֶךָ.
וְהָיוּ הַדְּבָרִים הָאֵלֶּה אֲשֶׁר אָנֹכִי מְצַוְּךָ הַיּוֹם עַל לְבָבֶךָ.

L'ma-an Tizk'ru (Numbers 15:40) (1 occurrence)

לְמַעַן תִּזְכְּרוּ וַעֲשִׂיתֶם אֶת כָּל מִצְוֹתָי וִהְיִיתֶם קְדֹשִׁים לֵאלֹהֵיכֶם.

From *Ahavah Rabbah* (1 occurrence)

וְהָאֵר עֵינֵינוּ בְּתוֹרָתֶךָ וְדַבֵּק לִבֵּנוּ בְּמִצְוֹתֶיךָ וְיַחֵד לְבָבֵנוּ
לְאַהֲבָה וּלְיִרְאָה אֶת שְׁמֶךָ.

From the Torah service (1 occurrence)

תּוֹרָה צִוָּה לָנוּ מֹשֶׁה

These are the block print forms of the Hebrew letters introduced in this chapter.

ָי ֹי   ַד ד   ץ ַצ   צ ָצ

These are their script forms.

ֹי י   ַדּ ד   ץ ַצ   צ ָצ

Hebrew Writing Exercises

1. Write a line of the letter *Tzadi*, using either block print or script.

_____ צ

2. Write a line of the letter *Tzadi Sofit* (Final *Tzadi*), using either block print or script.

_____ ץ

3. Write a line of the letter *Dalet*, using either block print or script.

_____ ד

4. Write a line of the letter *Yod*, using either block print or script.

_____ י

Exercises

1. Draw a line connecting each Hebrew consonant and vowel combination with the English word that has the same sound.

yachts	דִיל	meats	שְׂע
rude	יֶת	dome	יוֹר
dot	אֵיד	lie	בֶּצְ
yet	תֹד	shots	מִיץ
head	יַ֫צְ	votes	דֶצְ

deal	רוד	bets	וץ
aid	הֵד	your	לַי
toad	דָת	dates	דוֹם

2. Write the Hebrew consonant and vowel combinations that sound like the following English words. There may be more than one possible combination.

a. den _____

b. nets _____

c. yell _____

d. beets _____

e. sheets _____

f. hates _____

  _____

g. shade _____

h. roots _____

i. lewd _____

  _____

j. load _____

k. lots _____

l. nod _____

  _____

m. tie _____

n. my _____

o. shy _____

3. The following reading practice focuses on look-alike letters that can be easily confused. Read each combination aloud.

.a   דֵר הֵר הוֹד הוּד הוּךְ הוּץ הַץ דַץ רָץ

.b   צֵבָן צְבוּ צָנוּ אָבָן אֵכוּ אֶבוּ אָנוּ

.c   יְוְכָה יְוָנָה יַיִן יַן יַן מַן מוּ מֵי מִי

.d   אֵלֶיךָ אֵלַי אֵלִי צָלִי צַלִּי עֲלַי עָלַי

.e   רַבָּה רַכָּה רָב רוֹ רַן רַךְ רַד רֵד

.f   תָוַי תַּוָח תָּוָה הֶוְיָה תָּוֵי חַוֵּי חַיֵּי

.g   צִיּוֹן אַיִן שִׁין שִׁיךְ שִׁיֵץ שִׂיא שֵׂץ

.h   וַיִּךְ וַיְד יָדְה יָרַח יָדְה יוֹדֵה יוֹרֶה

.i   אֵיכָה אָבָה צֶבַע צָבָא צְנָה אָמָא

Try to read the following words in Hebrew first to see if you recognize them, before looking at the English translation.

David	—	דָּוִד
Miriam	—	מִרְיָם
bar mitzvah	—	בַּר מִצְוָה
bat mitzvah	—	בַּת מִצְוָה
unleavened bread	—	מַצָּה
sufficient for us	—	דַּיֵּנוּ
praise God!	—	הַלְלוּיָהּ
Jerusalem	—	יְרוּשָׁלַיִם
Zion	—	צִיּוֹן
prayer quorum of ten adult Jews	—	מִנְיָן
Rosh Chodesh (the new moon)	—	רֹאשׁ חֹדֶשׁ
distinction, separation (name of ceremony marking the end of Shabbat)	—	הַבְדָּלָה

forever and ever	—	לְעוֹלָם וָעֶד
the Evil Inclination	—	יֵצֶר הָרַע
ascent (immigration to Israel; the honor of being called to the Torah)	—	עֲלִיָּה
eternal light	—	נֵר תָּמִיד *candle*
Jew	—	יְהוּדִי
Judah	—	יְהוּדָה
standing (name of a portion of the worship service said while standing)	—	עֲמִידָה
household peace, family harmony	—	שְׁלוֹם בַּיִת

4. Read aloud the following letter and vowel combinations.

צָמִיד צָרִיךְ אָעִיר צָעִיר צַעַר צָעַד .a

דִּיצָה רִיצָה רָצָה רָאָה רוֹמֶה דּוֹמֶה .b

וֶרֶד וְרִדָּה וָעֶד וְדוֹר וִתּוּר וַעֲדָה .c

נִשְׁבַּץ נִשְׁבְּצָה מְשַׁבֵּץ שָׁבַץ שִׁבְצָה .d

יַד יָדַד יָדַיִם יָדִיד יְדִידוּת יְדִיעוֹת .e

חַיָּה חַיָּב חַיִל חַיֵּךְ חַיֶּיךָ בְּחַיֶּיךָ .f

מְכֻבָּד מְכֹעָר מְבֹעָר מְנֹעָר נוֹעָד .g

לֵיצָן לוֹצֵץ לָאֵץ לְכֵךְ לוֹנֵן הִתְלוֹנֵן .h

עֶדְרֵי עֲדָרַי עֲבָדִי עֲבָדֶיךָ עֶכְרָנֶיךָ .i

5. Read aloud the following words and phrases taken from the Bible and the prayer book.

Response to the *Bar'chu*

בָּרוּךְ יְיָ הַמְּבֹרָךְ לְעוֹלָם וָעֶד. .a

From the *V'ahavta* (Deuteronomy 6:6)

וְהָיוּ הַדְּבָרִים הָאֵלֶּה אֲשֶׁר אָנֹכִי מְצַוְּךָ הַיּוֹם עַל לְבָבֶךָ. .b

From the *V'ahavta* (Deuteronomy 6:7)

וְשִׁנַּנְתָּם לְבָנֶיךָ וְדִבַּרְתָּ בָּם בְּשִׁבְתְּךָ בְּבֵיתֶךָ וּבְלֶכְתְּךָ בַדֶּרֶךְ... .c

L'ma-an Tizk'ru (Numbers 15:41)

אֲנִי יְהוָֹה אֱלֹהֵיכֶם אֲשֶׁר הוֹצֵאתִי אֶתְכֶם .d
מֵאֶרֶץ מִצְרַיִם לִהְיוֹת לָכֶם לֵאלֹהִים.
אֲנִי יְהוָֹה אֱלֹהֵיכֶם.

From *Mi Chamochah* (Exodus 15:18)

יְהוָֹה יִמְלֹךְ לְעוֹלָם וָעֶד. .e

From *Hashkiveinu*

וּשְׁמוֹר צֵאתֵנוּ וּבוֹאֵנוּ לְחַיִּים וּלְשָׁלוֹם מֵעַתָּה וְעַד עוֹלָם .f

From the *Avot*

בָּרוּךְ אַתָּה יְיָ אֱלֹהֵינוּ וֵאלֹהֵי אֲבוֹתֵינוּ .g
וְאִמּוֹתֵינוּ, אֱלֹהֵי אַבְרָהָם ... אֱלֹהֵי לֵאָה וֵאלֹהֵי רָחֵל

From *R'tzei Vim'nuchateinu*

אֱלֹהֵינוּ וֵאלֹהֵי אֲבוֹתֵינוּ וְאִמּוֹתֵינוּ, רְצֵה בִמְנוּחָתֵנוּ... .h

From *Modim Anachnu*

מוֹדִים אֲנַחְנוּ לָךְ, שָׁאַתָּה הוּא יְיָ אֱלֹהֵינוּ .i
וֵאלֹהֵי אֲבוֹתֵינוּ וְאִמּוֹתֵינוּ לְעוֹלָם וָעֶד.
צוּר חַיֵּינוּ...

From the end of *Aleinu* (Zechariah 14:9)

בַּיּוֹם הַהוּא יִהְיֶה יְהֹוָה אֶחָד וּשְׁמוֹ אֶחָד. .j

The Number 18 and חַי

The letter ח is the eighth letter of the Hebrew alphabet; the letter י is the tenth. These two letters have the combined numerical value of eighteen. They also spell the Hebrew word חַי, which means "alive" or "living." For this reason, the number eighteen has become associated with "life" and the affirmation of life.

Many Jews make charitable donations in the amount of eighteen dollars, or multiples of eighteen. The giving of charity has long been regarded in the Jewish tradition as a life-affirming act for both the giver as well as the recipient. This view is reflected in Proverbs 10:2: צְדָקָה תַּצִּיל מִמָּוֶת—"Charity will save [one] from death." This idea is expounded upon in numerous passages in the rabbinic literature, such as the following talmudic excerpt:

"Rav Judah used to say: Ten strong things have been created in the world. Rock is hard, but iron cleaves it. Iron is hard, but fire softens it. Fire is powerful, but water quenches it. Water is heavy, but clouds bear it. Clouds are thick, but wind scatters them. Wind is strong, but a body resists it. The body is strong, but fear crushes it. Fear is powerful, but wine banishes it. Wine is strong, but sleep works it off. Death is stronger than all, yet charity saves from death." (*Bava Batra* 10a)

Review

You have now learned the following Hebrew letters.

ש ב ת ל מ ס ם ה ר

א ע נ ן ח כ ך ו ב

צ ץ ד י

You have learned sixteen vowel symbols.

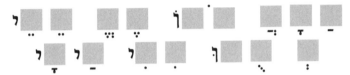

And you have learned eleven basic Jewish vocabulary words.

שַׁבָּת שָׁלוֹם תּוֹרָה שֵׁם שְׁמַע

בָּרוּךְ בְּרָכָה תְּשׁוּבָה אַהֲבָה

מִצְוָה חַיִּים

rest, cease from labor, desist	—	שׁ-ב-ת
complete, whole	—	שׁ-ל-ם
guard, keep, preserve	—	שׁ-מ-ר
give, grant, permit	—	נ-ת-ן
bless	—	ב-ר-ך
love, affection	—	א-ה-ב
command, order	—	צ-ו-ה

CHAPTER 8

74

This chapter introduces three new letters. One of them, the letter *Kaf*, was introduced in Chapter 5 without a dot in the middle. When it appears with a dot, it has the same sound as the letter *Kuf* also introduced here. The letter *Pei* is another letter whose pronunciation is altered by the presence or absence of a dot in the middle. This chapter introduces the letter *Pei* with a dot in the middle.

Pei (with a dot)	**p** as in **p**at	פּ
Kuf	**k** as in **k**ite	ק
Kaf (with a dot)	**k** as in **k**ite	כּ

Reading Practice

Say aloud the sounds of the following letters, which include those from previous chapters as well as the new letters. Say the word "silent" for those letters that are silent. Try to do this without looking at the chart above.

.a   פּ ק פֿ כ פּ ב ב כ כ כ ק ק כ ק

.b   י ק ר ד ד ך ז ו ו נ כ ב ב כ פּ

.c   פ כ ת ח ה ה י ד ק ע ע צ א

Read aloud the following letter and vowel combinations.

.d   קוֹ קוּ קִי קֵי פִי פֵּי כֶ פֶּ פָ כָּ קַ

.e   י צ ד׳ פוּ כוּ בוּ בְ כָ קִי פֵּי שָׂי

Read aloud the following single-syllable combinations.

.f   יֵק וַיק עֵק מֵק הֻפֵ חֻפֵ תֻפֵ רֻפֵ דֻפֵ

.g   צָק שֻק בֵק אוֹק צוֹק פוֹק דוֹק יוֹק

.h   פִיו פֵן קֵן פִים קים קַיא פֵיא כַּיא

.i   כַּב כַּנֶ כָּ פָֹך פוֹץ קוֹץ כֹה פֹה

Read aloud the following longer combinations of letters and vowels.

j. שֶׁקֶר בָּקָר בָּקַע פָּקַח פָּקַד

k. כָּבוֹד כּוֹאֵב כּוֹלֵל כּוֹלָם כֶּרֶם כֹּרֵחַ

l. מְנַקֵּב מְנַקֵּד נֶקֶד תֵּקֵד תִּקַּח לָקַח

m. פִּינוּ לַפִּידוֹת פֵּיוֹת פִּיצוּ פִּיצָה

n. אָאַפֵּץ אָאַפֵּק לְאָבֵק אָפֵק אָבֵק אָנֵק

o. קַו קָוָה קִיּוּמוֹ קִיּוּם קַם וְקַיָּם קַיָּם

p. פִּינְכֵּי פִּינָךְ אַפַּיִךְ אַיִךְ אֵיכָה כָּכָה

You have now learned the letters and vowels that spell another basic Jewish vocabulary word:

צְדָקָה

This word is most often translated as "charity," although that translation does not fully convey the meaning of the Hebrew. The word comes from the root צ-ד-ק, which has the basic meaning of "just" or "right." The act of giving *tzedakah* is regarded as an act of justice; all human beings are entitled to have their basic needs met, and those who have the means are obliged to help others. The Hebrew word for a righteous individual, a *tzaddik*, צַדִּיק, also comes from this root.

HEBREW Key Quote

Deuteronomy 16:20

A word from the root צ-ד-ק that has the meaning of "justice" appears in the following quote from the Torah. All but the last letter of this quote have been introduced.

צֶדֶק צֶדֶק תִּרְדֹּף.

Justice, justice, shall you pursue.

You have now learned all the basic Hebrew vowel sounds. In this chapter, and in the remaining chapters of this book, vowels will be introduced that appear much less frequently than those you have already learned. The two vowel symbols introduced in this chapter represent the same sound, which is like the sound of the וֹ vowel introduced in Chapter 2.

sounds like **o** as in flow	◌ָ or ◌ָ *(The ◌ represents any Hebrew letter.)*
sounds like **o** as in flow	◌ֳָ *(The ◌ represents any Hebrew letter.)*

In Chapter 1, you learned that the ◌ָ vowel has the sound of *ah* as in *father*. While this is true in the vast majority of cases, there are a few instances in which the ◌ָ vowel sounds like *o* as in *flow*. The most common Hebrew word in which this occurs is the word כָּל, which means "all" or "every." This word appears in many Hebrew phrases, prayers, and biblical passages, often with prefixes attached. Sometimes the dot is omitted from the letter *Kaf*, which changes the pronunciation of that letter, but does not affect the pronunciation of the ◌ָ vowel.

Read aloud the following.

מִכָּל כְּכָל לְכָל וּבְכָל בְּכָל וְכָל כָּל

שֶׁבְּכָל שֶׁכָּל וּמִכָּל וּלְכָל וּכְכָל

In general, when you encounter the ◌ָ vowel, it is probably best to pronounce it as *ah* unless you have been told otherwise or it appears in some form of the word כָּל. Some prayer books assist the reader in pronouncing this vowel by using a different symbol whenever the pronunciation is *oh*. The gender-sensitive edition of the prayer book *Gates of Prayer* uses the symbol ◌ָ. This book will use this symbol as well. Read aloud the following examples that utilize this symbol.

קָדְשׁוֹ קָדְשְׁךָ תְּחָנֵּנוּ בְּחָכְמָה וּבְשָׁכְבְּךָ

וְכָתְבֵנוּ אָכְלָם

The Combination Vowel ◌ֳָ

In Chapter 6, you learned the combination vowels ◌ֲ and ◌ֱ, formed by combining the ◌ְ vowel with the ◌ַ and ◌ֶ vowels. The combination vowel ◌ֳָ, introduced in this chapter, is formed by combining the ◌ְ vowel with the ◌ָ vowel, which sounds like *oh*. Therefore, the combination vowel ◌ֳָ is always pronounced *oh*. This vowel rarely appears in the prayer book. Read aloud the following words containing this vowel. Some of these words also utilize the ◌ָ symbol mentioned above.

עֳנִי אֳנִיָּה וְצָהֳרִים אֳהָלִי אָהֳבָם

You have now learned the letters that form a very common Hebrew root: ק-ד-שׁ. This root appears frequently in the prayer book and the Bible. The basic meaning of this root is "holy," "sacred," or "set apart" from the ordinary.

The root ק-ד-שׁ appears in the traditional wording of Hebrew blessings for the performance of a mitzvah. The performance of a mitzvah is thereby acknowledged as an act set apart from the ordinary, with the potential to raise the performer to a higher realm of holiness.

בָּרוּךְ אַתָּה יְיָ אֱלֹהֵינוּ מֶלֶךְ הָעוֹלָם, אֲשֶׁר קִדְּשָׁנוּ
בְּמִצְוֹתָיו, וְצִוָּנוּ...

Blessed are You, Eternal our God, Sovereign of the universe, who makes us holy with mitzvot and commands us ...

Following are other Hebrew words formed from the root ק-ד-שׁ. You can now read all the letters and vowels that appear in these words.

holy, sacred	—	קָדוֹשׁ
Kaddish (memorial prayer for the dead)	—	קַדִּישׁ
Kiddush (blessing sanctifying holy days said over wine) (*literally:* sanctification)	—	קִדּוּשׁ
holiness, sanctity	—	קְדֻשָׁה
holiness, sanctity	—	קֹדֶשׁ
Holy of Holies	—	קֹדֶשׁ הַקֳּדָשִׁים
martyrdom (*literally:* sanctification of the [Divine] Name)	—	קִדּוּשׁ הַשֵׁם
marriage	—	קִדּוּשִׁין
sexual figure identified with the cults that worshiped the pagan gods Ba'al and Astarte	—	קְדֵשָׁה

Try to find the root ק-ד-שׁ in each of the following prayer book excerpts. The number of occurrences in each excerpt is indicated in parentheses. In most cases, prefixes and/or suffixes are attached.

L'ma-an Tizk'ru (Numbers 15:40) (1 occurrence)

לְמַעַן תִּזְכְּרוּ וַעֲשִׂיתֶם אֶת כָּל מִצְוֹתָי וִהְיִיתֶם קְדֹשִׁים לֵאלֹהֵיכֶם.

Mi Chamochah (1 occurrence)

מִי כָמֹכָה בָּאֵלִם יְיָ, מִי כָּמֹכָה נֶאְדָּר בַּקֹּדֶשׁ

R'tzei Vimnuchateinu (4 occurrences)

אֱלֹהֵינוּ וֵאלֹהֵי אֲבוֹתֵינוּ וְאִמּוֹתֵינוּ, רְצֵה בִמְנוּחָתֵנוּ. קַדְּשֵׁנוּ
בְּמִצְוֹתֶיךָ וְתֵן חֶלְקֵנוּ בְּתוֹרָתֶךָ. שַׂבְּעֵנוּ מִטּוּבֶךָ, וְשַׂמְּחֵנוּ
בִּישׁוּעָתֶךָ, וְטַהֵר לִבֵּנוּ לְעָבְדְּךָ בֶּאֱמֶת. וְהַנְחִילֵנוּ יְיָ אֱלֹהֵינוּ,
בְּאַהֲבָה וּבְרָצוֹן שַׁבַּת קָדְשֶׁךָ, וְיָנוּחוּ בָהּ יִשְׂרָאֵל מְקַדְּשֵׁי
שְׁמֶךָ. בָּרוּךְ אַתָּה יְיָ, מְקַדֵּשׁ הַשַּׁבָּת.

Shabbat evening Kiddush (6 occurrences)

בָּרוּךְ אַתָּה יְיָ אֱלֹהֵינוּ מֶלֶךְ הָעוֹלָם, אֲשֶׁר קִדְּשָׁנוּ בְּמִצְוֹתָיו
וְרָצָה בָנוּ, וְשַׁבַּת קָדְשׁוֹ בְּאַהֲבָה וּבְרָצוֹן הִנְחִילָנוּ, זִכָּרוֹן
לְמַעֲשֵׂה בְרֵאשִׁית. כִּי הוּא יוֹם תְּחִלָּה לְמִקְרָאֵי קֹדֶשׁ, זֵכֶר
לִיצִיאַת מִצְרָיִם. כִּי בָנוּ בָחַרְתָּ וְאוֹתָנוּ קִדַּשְׁתָּ מִכָּל הָעַמִּים,
וְשַׁבַּת קָדְשְׁךָ בְּאַהֲבָה וּבְרָצוֹן הִנְחַלְתָּנוּ.
בָּרוּךְ אַתָּה יְיָ, מְקַדֵּשׁ הַשַּׁבָּת.

These are the block print forms of the Hebrew letters introduced in this chapter.

פ פּ ק קּ כ בּ

These are their script forms.

פ פּ ק קּ כ בּ

Hebrew Writing Exercises

1. Write a line of the letter *Pei* (with a dot), using either block print or script.

_____ פּ

2. Write a line of the letter *Kuf*, using either block print or script.

_____ ק

3. Write a line of the letter *Kaf* (with a dot), using either block print or script.

_____ כּ

Exercises

1. Draw a line connecting each Hebrew consonant and vowel combination with the English word that has the same sound.

knock	כְּפֵ	chic	יוֹק	
deck	אֵיק	cob	מָק	
quiche	כּוֹד	cool	פֵּב	
ache	דֶּכְ	coats	כַּבְּ	
keep	פְּל	yoke	פֵּן	
peeve	נָק	mock	קֹץ	
code	פִּיו	pen	שֶׁכְּ	
pool	קִישׁ	pave	כּוּל	

2. The following Hebrew combinations sound like real English words in sentences.
   Read aloud.

שִׂיא כֶּם תֶּע מַי הוֹם.

אַי יֶל: "לֶץ אִית!"

שִׂיא עֶת מַי מִית.

שִׂיא עֶת מַי אוֹץ.

שִׂיא עֶת מַי פַּי.

שִׂיא עֶת מַי כֵּיק.

שִׂיא לֶת מִי קִיפּ מַי בִּיץ.

אַי דֶע נַת אִית בִּיץ.

3. Write the Hebrew consonant and vowel combinations that sound like the following English
   words. There is more than one possibility for each word.

   a. peck _____   **b.** pie _____   **c.** pain _____

   _____   _____   _____

   d. cane _____   **e.** comb _____   **f.** key _____

   _____   _____   _____

   g. lock _____   **h.** deep _____   **i.** heap _____

   _____   _____   _____

   j. hoop _____   **k.** oak _____   **l.** bop _____

   _____   _____   _____

4. The following reading practice focuses on look-alike letters that can be easily confused. Read
   each combination aloud.

a. פִּיו   פִּין   פִּיך   פִּיַד   פִּיר   כִּיר   בִּיַר

b. תָּק   חָק   הָק   בוֹק   כוֹק   כוֹק   בוֹק

c. יָפּ   וָפּ   נָפּ   כָפּ   פוֹב   פוֹכ   פוֹן   פוֹץ

Try to read the following words first in Hebrew to see if you recognize them before looking at the English translation.

cap, yarmulke	—	כִּפָּה	
Chanukah (dedication)	—	חֲנֻכָּה	
Yom Kippur (Day of Atonement)	—	יוֹם כִּפּוּר	
Isaac	—	יִצְחָק	
Rebecca	—	רִבְקָה	
Jacob	—	יַעֲקֹב	
kosher	—	כָּשֵׁר	
kibbutz	—	קִבּוּץ	
Kol Nidrei	—	כָּל נִדְרֵי	

wisdom	—	חָכְמָה
chupah (wedding canopy)	—	חֻפָּה
Purim	—	פּוּרִים
the Holy Ark	—	אֲרוֹן הַקֹּדֶשׁ
family	—	מִשְׁפָּחָה
marriage certificate	—	כְּתֻבָּה
the weekly Torah portion	—	פָּרָשַׁת הַשָּׁבוּעַ
repair of the world	—	תִּקּוּן עוֹלָם

5. Read aloud the following letter and vowel combinations.

a. שִׁכּוּן שִׁכּוֹר שְׁכוּנָה שִׁכּוֹר שָׁכַח

b. קַוֶּה תִּקְוָה הַתִּקְוָה קֶבַע קִבְעָה

c. פּוֹעֲלִי פָּעֳלִי פָּעֳלֵךְ פָּעֳלִי פָּעֳלִי

d. אִכָּר אִכָּרִי כִּכָּר כִּכְּרוֹתַי כְּכַרְכֶם

e. צָפָה צֻפָּה צִפִּיָּה מִצְפֶּה צְפִיּוֹת

f. דַּקּוֹת יַקּוּת יַקְרוּת דִּקְדוּק דַּקְדְקָן

g. מָצָא אֶמְצַע אֶמְצָעִי בָּאֶמְצָה עֹמֶץ

h. עֹמֶק עֲמֻקָּה הֶעֱמִיק הֶאֱמִיץ אַמִּיץ

i. כַּפִּית כַּפִּיּוֹת כַּפּוֹן כַּפּוֹנִי כַּפּוֹנֶיךָ

6. The following prayer book excerpts all contain some form of the word כָּל. Read aloud.

From *Kol Nidrei*

‏a. כָּל נִדְרֵי...

From *Nishmat Kol Chai*

‏b. נִשְׁמַת כָּל חַי תְּבָרֵךְ אֶת שִׁמְךָ...

From the *V'ahavta* (Deuteronomy 6:5)

‏c. וְאָהַבְתָּ אֵת יְהֹוָה אֱלֹהֶיךָ, בְּכָל לְבָבְךָ...
וּבְכָל מְאֹדֶךָ.

From the *K'dushah* (Isaiah 6:3)

‏d. קָדוֹשׁ, קָדוֹשׁ, קָדוֹשׁ, יְהֹוָה צְבָאוֹת, מְלֹא כָל הָאָרֶץ כְּבוֹדוֹ.

From the Torah service (Psalm 145:13)

‏e. מַלְכוּתְךָ מַלְכוּת כָּל עֹלָמִים, וּמֶמְשַׁלְתְּךָ בְּכָל דּוֹר וָדוֹר.

Blessing before the Torah reading

‏f. בָּרוּךְ אַתָּה יְיָ אֱלֹהֵינוּ מֶלֶךְ הָעוֹלָם,
אֲשֶׁר בָּחַר בָּנוּ מִכָּל הָעַמִּים וְנָתַן לָנוּ
אֶת תּוֹרָתוֹ. בָּרוּךְ אַתָּה יְיָ, נוֹתֵן הַתּוֹרָה.

From the blessing after the Haftarah reading

‏g. בָּרוּךְ אַתָּה יְיָ אֱלֹהֵינוּ מֶלֶךְ הָעוֹלָם, צוּר
כָּל הָעוֹלָמִים, צַדִּיק בְּכָל הַדּוֹרוֹת, הָאֵל
הַנֶּאֱמָן ... הַמְדַבֵּר וּמְקַיֵּם, שֶׁכָּל דְּבָרָיו אֱמֶת וָצֶדֶק.

The end of *Aleinu* (Zechariah 14:9)

‏h. וְנֶאֱמַר וְהָיָה יְהֹוָה לְמֶלֶךְ עַל כָּל הָאָרֶץ
בַּיּוֹם הַהוּא יִהְיֶה יְהֹוָה אֶחָד וּשְׁמוֹ אֶחָד.

CHAPTER 8

7. Read aloud the following excerpts from the prayer book.

Shabbat candle lighting blessing

.a בָּרוּךְ אַתָּה יְיָ אֱלֹהֵינוּ מֶלֶךְ הָעוֹלָם,
אֲשֶׁר קִדְּשָׁנוּ בְּמִצְוֹתָיו, וְצִוָּנוּ לְהַדְלִיק נֵר שֶׁל שַׁבָּת.

Blessing over bread

.b בָּרוּךְ אַתָּה יְיָ אֱלֹהֵינוּ מֶלֶךְ הָעוֹלָם, הַמּוֹצִיא לֶחֶם מִן הָאָרֶץ.

From *L'chah Dodi*

.c לְכָה דוֹדִי לִקְרַאת כַּלָּה פְּנֵי שַׁבָּת נְקַבְּלָה.

From *Mi Chamochah*

.d מִי כָמֹכָה בָּאֵלִם יְיָ, מִי כָּמֹכָה נֶאְדָּר בַּקֹּדֶשׁ...?

Baruch Shem

.e בָּרוּךְ שֵׁם כְּבוֹד מַלְכוּתוֹ לְעוֹלָם וָעֶד.

From *Ahavah Rabbah*

.f וְהָאֵר עֵינֵינוּ בְּתוֹרָתֶךָ, וְדַבֵּק לִבֵּנוּ בְּמִצְוֹתֶיךָ,
וְיַחֵד לְבָבֵנוּ לְאַהֲבָה וּלְיִרְאָה אֶת שְׁמֶךָ.

From *G'vurot*

.g מְכַלְכֵּל חַיִּים בְּחֶסֶד, מְחַיֵּה הַכֹּל בְּרַחֲמִים רַבִּים ...
וְנֶאֱמָן אַתָּה לְהַחֲיוֹת הַכֹּל. בָּרוּךְ אַתָּה יְיָ, מְחַיֵּה הַכֹּל.

From the *K'dushah* (Psalm 146:10)

.h יִמְלֹךְ יְהֹוָה לְעוֹלָם, אֱלֹהַיִךְ צִיּוֹן לְדֹר וָדֹר, הַלְלוּיָהּ.

From the Torah service (Isaiah 2:3; Micah 4:2)

.i כִּי מִצִּיּוֹן תֵּצֵא תוֹרָה, וּדְבַר יְהֹוָה מִירוּשָׁלָיִם.

From the Torah service

.j בָּרוּךְ שֶׁנָּתַן תּוֹרָה לְעַמּוֹ יִשְׂרָאֵל בִּקְדֻשָּׁתוֹ.

EXTRA CREDIT

The Kaddish

The *Kaddish*, which many people associate today with death and mourning, originated in talmudic times as a prayer said at the conclusion of a discourse or sermon in the house of study. It was the practice to conclude such a discourse with words of hope; hence the *Kaddish* speaks of the sanctification of the Divine Name and expresses the hope that we may witness the realm of God on earth. The opening words of the *Kaddish*, יִתְגַּדַּל וְיִתְקַדַּשׁ, echo the words of the prophet Ezekiel:

וְהִתְגַּדִּלְתִּי וְהִתְקַדִּשְׁתִּי וְנוֹדַעְתִּי לְעֵינֵי גּוֹיִם רַבִּים וְיָדְעוּ
כִּי־אֲנִי יְהֹוָה.

Thus will I magnify Myself and sanctify Myself, and I will make Myself known in the eyes of many nations; and they shall know that I am the Eternal. (Ezekiel 38:23)

Over time, the *Kaddish* came to be used not just at the conclusion of a study session, but also at the conclusion of the major sections of a prayer service. Various forms of the *Kaddish* exist; one of these is the shorter form known as the חֲצִי קַדִּישׁ or Half *Kaddish*, commonly referred to as the Reader's *Kaddish*.

The *Kaddish* came to be associated with mourners in the Middle Ages, at the time of the persecutions that accompanied the Crusades. It was thought that the uttering of this prayer by the living on behalf of the dead would benefit their souls and assure their salvation. Since the *Kaddish* is a prayer that can be said only in the presence of a minyan (the quorum of ten adult Jews required for the recitation of certain public prayers), saying *Kaddish* is an act that assures a mourner of the surrounding presence of a supportive community.

Though it is written with Hebrew letters and contains some Hebrew words, the *Kaddish* is mostly in Aramaic, which was the spoken language of the Jewish people in talmudic times. Aramaic is a sister Semitic language to Hebrew and shares many of the same word roots. The following are some Aramaic words from the *Kaddish* and the corresponding Hebrew words or roots that you have already learned:

a form of שֵׁם (name)	— שְׁמֵהּ	יְהֵא שְׁמֵהּ רַבָּא
(blessed) ב-ר-ך	— מְבָרַךְ	מְבָרַךְ לְעָלַם וּלְעָלְמֵי עָלְמַיָּא.
(blessed) ב-ר-ך	— יִתְבָּרַךְ	יִתְבָּרַךְ וְיִשְׁתַּבַּח וְיִתְפָּאַר...
(blessed) בָּרוּךְ	— בְּרִיךְ	בְּרִיךְ הוּא...
a form of בְּרָכָה (blessing)	— בִּרְכָתָא	מִן כָּל בִּרְכָתָא וְשִׁירָתָא...

Review

You have now learned the following Hebrew letters.

ש ב ת ל מ ס מ ה ר

א ע נ ז ח כ ך ו ב

צ ץ ד י כ ק פ

You have learned eighteen vowel symbols.

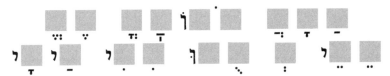

And you have learned twelve basic Jewish vocabulary words.

שַׁבָּת שָׁלוֹם תּוֹרָה שֵׁם שְׁמַע

בָּרוּךְ בְּרָכָה תְּשׁוּבָה אַהֲבָה

מִצְוָה חַיִּים צְדָקָה

rest, cease from labor, desist	—	שׁ-ב-ת
complete, whole	—	שׁ-ל-ם
guard, keep, preserve	—	שׁ-מ-ר
give, grant, permit	—	נ-ת-ן
bless	—	ב-ר-ך
love, affection	—	א-ה-ב
command, order	—	צ-ו-ה
holy, sacred, set apart	—	ק-ד-שׁ

This chapter introduces three new letters. The letter *Shin* was introduced in Chapter 1 with a dot above the right side of the letter, having the sound of *sh* as in *ship*. When the dot appears above the left side of the letter, it has the sound of *s* as in *sit* and is usually called *Sin* instead of *Shin*. The letter *Samech* has the same sound as the letter *Sin*. The letter *Pei* was introduced in Chapter 8 with a dot in the middle. This chapter introduces the sound of the letter *Pei* without a dot. The letter *Pei* also has a final form, which always appears without a dot in the middle.

Sin	s as in sit	שׂ
Samech	s as in sit	ס
Pei (without dot)	f as in fish	פ
Pei Sofit (Final *Pei*, without dot)	f as in fish	ף

Look-Alike Letters

The letters *Samech* and *Mem Sofit* (Final *Mem*) are virtually identical in appearance, except for the bottom corners. (In some Hebrew print styles only the bottom of the right corner letter *Samech* is rounded, while the left corner is squared-off like the corners of the *Mem Sofit*.) The letter *Samech* can appear in any position within a word, but *Mem Sofit* can appear only as the last letter.

Reading Practice

Say aloud the sounds of the following letters, which include some from previous chapters as well as the new letters. Try to do this without looking at the chart above.

a. שׁ שׂ ס שׂ ס ם ס ם מ פ ס ס ף

b. ף ר ק צ ץ ף ז ר ף פ ף ז

c. כ ק ף פ פ כ ד ס ם שׁ שׂ שׁ

Read aloud the following letter and vowel combinations.

d. שׁוֹ סוּ סוֹ שׁוּ שִׁי שֵׁ פֵּ פִּי פַּי פּוֹ פָ

e. פֶּ פַּ סֶ שׁ שֵׁ פּ פֵּ פַּ פָּ סֹ סֵ פִּי

Read aloud the following single-syllable combinations.

f. סוּף תֹּף עוֹף עָף כַּף נָף דִּיף לִיף

g. שׁוּם שׁוֹם סוּס מָס מֶשׁ כֵּישׁ קֶס יֶס

h. פִּץ פֵּץ פַּץ לֶץ לֵץ סֶץ סָף סֶךְ סִי

i. פֵּיא פִיא פֵּר פֶּב סֵב סָף חָף חוֹף

Read aloud the following longer combinations of letters and vowels.

j. נָפַל אָפַל חָפַל שָׁפַל כָּפַל סָפַל

k. סְעִיף סָרִיף צְרִיף חָרִיף וַרִיף שָׁרִיף

l. סִדּוּר סִפּוּר סָבוּר סָחוּר סָמוּר סָקוּר

m. מְבַשֵּׁר מְבַסֵּם מְבַסֵּס מְבַלֵּס מְבַלֵּם

n. צוֹפֶה רוֹפֵא נוֹפֶה סוֹפֶה יוֹפֶה תּוֹפֶה

o. אֶשְׂחַק אֲשַׂעֵר יְשַׂעֵר יְשַׂעֲרוּ יְשַׂחֲקוּ

p. יָשִׂישׂ יָשׂוּךְ יָשׂוֹר יִשְׂרוֹר יִשְׂרוֹן יִשְׂרַץ

You have learned the letters and vowels that spell another basic Jewish vocabulary word:

תְּפִלָה

This is the Hebrew word for "prayer." It comes from the root פ-ל-ל, which has the meanings of "judge" and "think" in addition to the meaning "supplicate" or "entreat." Thus, prayer in Hebrew encompasses a broad range of inner experience, including self-examination and reflection, in addition to reaching out to the One beyond oneself.

From the High Holiday liturgy

HEBREW Key Quote

The following excerpt is from the *Unetaneh Tokef* prayer in the the High Holy Day liturgy. Notice that it contains the words תְּפִלָּה, תְּשׁוּבָה, and צְדָקָה—all of which have been introduced in this book—with the prefix וּ attached. All but two letters in the last word of this quote have been introduced.

וּתְשׁוּבָה וּתְפִלָּה וּצְדָקָה מַעֲבִירִין אֶת רֹעַ הַגְּזֵרָה.

But repentance and prayer and charity cancel the severity of the decree.

This chapter does not introduce a new vowel sound. Instead it introduces an exception to the usual way of pronouncing vowel and consonant combinations. When the letter ח appears as the last letter of a word and has the vowel ◌ַ written under it, the vowel is sounded before the consonant, instead of the usual pronunciation of the Hebrew vowel sound after the consonant. Words that end in חַ are usually accented on the syllable preceding the חַ.

sounds like **cha** (ch as in Ba**ch**)	חַ	*at the beginning or in the middle of a word*
sounds like **ach** (ch as in Ba**ch**)	חַ	*at the end of a word*

 Reading Practice

a. שִׂיחַ רוּחַ לוּחַ מוֹחַ אוֹרֵחַ בּוֹרֵחַ יָרֵחַ

b. מְשַׁלֵּחַ מְפַיֵּחַ הָאָנָח הֲרֵקַח הַקֶּפַח

c. וִכּוּחַ חִתּוּכֵחַ קוֹרֵחַ סוֹלֵחַ לְאָרֹחַ

d. מַבְרִיחַ שָׁלִיחַ מַצְוֹיֵחַ מִצְנָח מִשְׁלוֹחַ

Key Phrases from Jewish Life

There are two phrases commonly used in Jewish religious life that contain the חַ ending introduced above. One is the greeting used on festivals and holidays other than Shabbat. (The last letter of the first word has not yet been introduced.)

חַג שָׂמֵחַ—Happy holiday!

The other is the words of encouragement offered in the synagogue to one who has received a ritual honor, such as being called to the Torah for an *aliyah* (the honor of saying the blessings before and after the Torah reading):

Well done! *or* More power to you! — יְיַשֵׁר כֹּחַ

(*literally:* May [your] strength be upright.)

You can now read another basic Jewish vocabulary word, which comes from the same root as the word שָׂמֵחַ in the Hebrew expression above:

שִׂמְחָה

This is a noun meaning "rejoicing" or "happiness." It appears in several passages in the prayer book and in many holiday songs. This word is also used sometimes to mean "a joyous occasion." In this sense, one can hear the word used to refer to the celebrations surrounding joyous life-cycle events such as baby-namings or weddings.

THE ROOT ע-שׂ-ה

You have now learned the letters that form a very common Hebrew root: ע-שׂ-ה. This root has the basic meaning of "make" or "do" or "act." It appears frequently in the prayer book and in the Bible.

The following are examples of Hebrew words or phrases formed from the root ע-שׂ-ה. When the letter ה is the last letter of a root, it sometimes does not appear in words formed from that root. In some of the examples below, the letter ה has dropped out and only the root letters שׂ and ע remain.

deed, act, story	—	מַעֲשֶׂה
practical, feasible, workable	—	מַעֲשִׂי
tale, legend, fairy-tale	—	מַעֲשִׂיָּה
practicability, feasibility	—	מַעֲשִׂיּוּת
Creation, the act (mystery) of Creation	—	מַעֲשֵׂה בְרֵאשִׁית
actually, in fact	—	לְמַעֲשֶׂה
there's nothing to be done; it can't be helped	—	אֵין מַה לַעֲשׂוֹת
industry, manufacture	—	תַּעֲשִׂיָּה

Try to find the root ע-שׂ-ה in each of the following prayer book excerpts. The number of occurrences of the root in each excerpt is indicated in parentheses. In some cases, the letter ה has dropped out and only the root letters שׂ and ע remain. In most cases, prefixes and/or suffixes are attached.

L'ma-an Tizk'ru (Numbers 15:40) (1 occurrence)

לְמַעַן תִּזְכְּרוּ וַעֲשִׂיתֶם אֶת כָּל מִצְוֹתָי וִהְיִיתֶם קְדֹשִׁים לֵאלֹהֵיכֶם.

Shabbat evening *Kiddush* (1 occurrence)

בָּרוּךְ אַתָּה יְיָ אֱלֹהֵינוּ מֶלֶךְ הָעוֹלָם, אֲשֶׁר קִדְּשָׁנוּ בְּמִצְוֹתָיו וְרָצָה בָנוּ, וְשַׁבַּת קָדְשׁוֹ בְּאַהֲבָה וּבְרָצוֹן הִנְחִילָנוּ, זִכָּרוֹן לְמַעֲשֵׂה בְרֵאשִׁית.

Adon Olam (1 occurrence)

אֲדוֹן עוֹלָם אֲשֶׁר מָלַךְ, בְּטֶרֶם כָּל יְצִיר נִבְרָא. לְעֵת נַעֲשָׂה בְחֶפְצוֹ כֹּל, אֲזַי מֶלֶךְ שְׁמוֹ נִקְרָא

Second blessing for lighting Chanukah candles (1 occurrence)

בָּרוּךְ אַתָּה יְיָ אֱלֹהֵינוּ מֶלֶךְ הָעוֹלָם, שֶׁעָשָׂה נִסִּים לַאֲבוֹתֵינוּ בַּיָּמִים הָהֵם בַּזְּמַן הַזֶּה.

Yotzer (6 occurrences)

בָּרוּךְ אַתָּה יְיָ, אֱלֹהֵינוּ, מֶלֶךְ הָעוֹלָם, יוֹצֵר אוֹר וּבוֹרֵא חֹשֶׁךְ, עֹשֶׂה שָׁלוֹם וּבוֹרֵא אֶת הַכֹּל. הַמֵּאִיר לָאָרֶץ וְלַדָּרִים עָלֶיהָ בְּרַחֲמִים, וּבְטוּבוֹ מְחַדֵּשׁ בְּכָל יוֹם תָּמִיד מַעֲשֵׂה בְרֵאשִׁית. מָה רַבּוּ מַעֲשֶׂיךָ, יְיָ! כֻּלָּם בְּחָכְמָה עָשִׂיתָ, מָלְאָה הָאָרֶץ קִנְיָנֶךָ: תִּתְבָּרַךְ, יְיָ אֱלֹהֵינוּ, עַל שֶׁבַח מַעֲשֵׂה יָדֶיךָ. וְעַל מְאוֹרֵי אוֹר שֶׁעָשִׂיתָ. יְפָאֲרוּךָ סֶּלָה.

These are the block print forms of the Hebrew letters introduced in this chapter.

These are their script forms.

ﭏ ﭏ ﭏ ﭏ ﭏ ﭏ

Hebrew Writing Exercises

1. Write a line of the letter *Sin* (with the dot on the left), using either block print or script.

_____ שׂ

2. Write a line of the letter *Samech*, using either block print or script.

_____ ס

3. Write a line of the letter *Pei* (without a dot), using either block print or script.

_____ פ

4. Write a line of the letter *Pei Sofit* (Final *Pei*), using either block print or script.

_____ ף

Exercises

1. Draw a line connecting each Hebrew consonant and vowel combination with the English word that has the same sound.

moose	פֶשׂ	sets		פַּר
beef	סִי	loaf		שֵׂד
chef	פוֹן	far		רֶף
face	נִישׂ	feign		לֵף
sock	בִּף	seed		סְפֵּ
phone	מֶשׂ	save		שֵׂוֹ

sigh	סָק	roof	סָ֫ף
niece	שִׁף	soup	פָּן

2. The following Hebrew combinations sound like real English words in sentences. Read aloud.

אַי הוֹפּ יֶע דוּ נַת סִי מַי רוּם.

יֶע הֵית תוּ סִי מַי רוּם.

"פֶה!" יֶע שִׁיה.

"אַי סִי פְּד אָן יוּר בֶּד.

יוּר בּוּץ אַר אָן יוּר בֶּד.

אַי דוּ נַת סִי שִׁיץ אָן יוּר בֶּד."

"יֶס," אַי סַי.

"אַי נִיד לֶשׁ מֶשׂ!"

3. Write the Hebrew consonant and vowel combinations that sound like the following English words. There may be more than one possible combination.

a. fake _____

_____

b. fame _____

_____

c. foam _____

_____

d. soap _____

_____

e. scene _____

_____

f. sell _____

_____

g. sod _____

_____

h. off _____

_____

i. deaf _____

_____

j. poof _____

_____

k. cease _____

_____

l. lace _____

_____

4. The following reading practice focuses on look-alike letters that can be easily confused. Read each combination aloud.

a. חוּס חוֹם שׁוֹם שָׁס שָׁם שָׂמָה שָׁם

b. חוֹף תָף חָפָּה סוֹפָה צִיף אִיף אִיץ

c. פְּק פֵּק פֶּךְ פֶּךְ פֶּךְ פֵּץ פֶּץ פִּיס פִּים

Try to read the following words in Hebrew first to see if you recognize them before looking at the English translation.

Sarah	—	שָׂרָה
Joseph	—	יוֹסֵף
shofar	—	שׁוֹפָר
Israel	—	יִשְׂרָאֵל
sukkah	—	סֻכָּה
Sukkot	—	סֻכּוֹת
Passover	—	פֶּסַח
Simchat Torah	—	שִׂמְחַת תּוֹרָה
seder (*literally:* order, arrangement)	—	סֵדֶר
prayer book	—	סִדּוּר
tefillin, phylacteries	—	תְּפִלִּין
Torah scroll	—	סֵפֶר תּוֹרָה
synagogue	—	בֵּית כְּנֶסֶת
saving a life	—	פִּקוּחַ נֶפֶשׁ

---

5. Read aloud the following letter and vowel combinations.

a. קָצַף רָצַף שָׁתָף שַׁחַף דָחַף שָׂכָף

b. יָנוּחַ יָדוּחַ יָסִיחַ לְשׂוֹחֵחַ יַדְלִיחַ יַאֲרִיחַ

c. שָׂשׂוֹן סַבּוֹן צָפוֹן קָפַץ אָפַץ אָפוֹה

d. שֵׁיבָה שֵׂיָה שִׂכְוִי שְׁחִיָה שָׁכֵן סַכִּין

e. מִסְבָּךְ מְסֻבִּין מִסָּבִיב מְסֻדָּר מְשֻׁדָּד

f. לְפָנַי כַּפֵּי שָׂרֵי מַעֲשֵׂי שַׁדַּי שְׂפָתַי

g. נֶאֱסַף נֶאֱכַף נֶהֱרַס נֶאֱפַס נָפַל

h. סָאֲבָה שְׁאֵרָה פְּאֵרָה מְפֹאָר מְסֹאָר

i. מְנַצֵּחַ מְפַצֵּחַ מְצֻלָּח מְשֻׂמֵּחַ מְפֻסֵּחַ

6. The following prayer book excerpts all contain a word with the ַה ending. Read aloud.

From the *Aleinu*

a. עָלֵינוּ לְשַׁבֵּחַ לַאֲדוֹן הַכֹּל...

From *Ashrei* (Psalm 145:16)

b. פּוֹתֵחַ אֶת יָדֶךָ, וּמַשְׂבִּיעַ לְכָל חַי רָצוֹן.

From the Morning Blessings

c. בָּרוּךְ אַתָּה יְיָ אֱלֹהֵינוּ מֶלֶךְ הָעוֹלָם, פּוֹקֵחַ עִוְרִים.

From *Ma'ariv Aravim*

d. בָּרוּךְ אַתָּה יְיָ, אֱלֹהֵינוּ מֶלֶךְ הָעוֹלָם,
אֲשֶׁר בִּדְבָרוֹ מַעֲרִיב עֲרָבִים, בְּחָכְמָה
פּוֹתֵחַ שְׁעָרִים, וּבִתְבוּנָה מְשַׁנֶּה עִתִּים...

From *G'vurot*

e. מְכַלְכֵּל חַיִּים בְּחֶסֶד, מְחַיֵּה הַכֹּל בְּרַחֲמִים רַבִּים.
סוֹמֵךְ נוֹפְלִים, וְרוֹפֵא חוֹלִים, וּמַתִּיר אֲסוּרִים,
וּמְקַיֵּם אֱמוּנָתוֹ לִישֵׁנֵי עָפָר. מִי כָמוֹךָ...
וּמִי דּוֹמֶה לָךְ, מֶלֶךְ מֵמִית וּמְחַיֶּה וּמַצְמִיחַ יְשׁוּעָה?
וְנֶאֱמָן אַתָּה לְהַחֲיוֹת הַכֹּל. בָּרוּךְ אַתָּה יְיָ, מְחַיֵּה הַכֹּל.

CHAPTER 9

7. Read aloud the following excerpts from the prayer book.

The *Shema* (Deuteronomy 6:4)

a. שְׁמַע יִשְׂרָאֵל, יְהוָֹה אֱלֹהֵינוּ, יְהוָֹה אֶחָד.

From *Yihyu L'ratzon* (Psalm 19:15)

b. יִהְיוּ לְרָצוֹן אִמְרֵי פִי...

From *V'ahavta* (Deuteronomy 6:5)

c. וְאָהַבְתָּ אֵת יְהוָֹה אֱלֹהֶיךָ בְּכָל לְבָבְךָ
וּבְכָל נַפְשְׁךָ וּבְכָל מְאֹדֶךָ.

Oseh Shalom

d. עֹשֶׂה שָׁלוֹם בִּמְרוֹמָיו, הוּא יַעֲשֶׂה שָׁלוֹם
עָלֵינוּ וְעַל כָּל יִשְׂרָאֵל, וְאִמְרוּ אָמֵן.

Mi Chamochah (Exodus 15:11)

e. מִי כָמֹכָה בָּאֵלִם יְהוָֹה, מִי כָּמֹכָה נֶאְדָּר
בַּקֹּדֶשׁ, נוֹרָא תְהִלֹּת, עֹשֵׂה פֶלֶא?

V'shamru (Exodus 31:16–17)

f. וְשָׁמְרוּ בְנֵי יִשְׂרָאֵל אֶת הַשַּׁבָּת, לַעֲשׂוֹת
אֶת הַשַּׁבָּת לְדֹרֹתָם בְּרִית עוֹלָם. בֵּינִי
וּבֵין בְּנֵי יִשְׂרָאֵל אוֹת הִיא לְעֹלָם, כִּי
שֵׁשֶׁת יָמִים עָשָׂה יְהוָֹה אֶת הַשָּׁמַיִם וְאֶת
הָאָרֶץ, וּבַיּוֹם הַשְּׁבִיעִי שָׁבַת וַיִּנָּפַשׁ.

From *L'chah Dodi*

g. לְכָה דוֹדִי לִקְרַאת כַּלָּה, פְּנֵי שַׁבָּת נְקַבְּלָה ...
לִקְרַאת שַׁבָּת לְכוּ וְנֵלְכָה, כִּי הִיא מְקוֹר הַבְּרָכָה.
מֵרֹאשׁ מִקֶּדֶם נְסוּכָה, סוֹף מַעֲשֶׂה, בְּמַחֲשָׁבָה תְּחִלָּה.

Vay'chulu (Genesis 2:1–3)

h. וַיְכֻלּוּ הַשָּׁמַיִם וְהָאָרֶץ וְכָל צְבָאָם. וַיְכַל אֱלֹהִים
בַּיּוֹם הַשְּׁבִיעִי, מְלַאכְתּוֹ אֲשֶׁר עָשָׂה, וַיִּשְׁבֹּת בַּיּוֹם הַשְּׁבִיעִי,
מִכָּל מְלַאכְתּוֹ אֲשֶׁר עָשָׂה. וַיְבָרֶךְ אֱלֹהִים
אֶת יוֹם הַשְּׁבִיעִי וַיְקַדֵּשׁ אֹתוֹ, כִּי בוֹ
שָׁבַת מִכָּל מְלַאכְתּוֹ, אֲשֶׁר בָּרָא אֱלֹהִים לַעֲשׂוֹת.

From the Torah service (Psalms 86:8; 145:13; Exodus 15:18)

i. אֵין כָּמוֹךָ בָאֱלֹהִים, אֲדֹנָי, וְאֵין כְּמַעֲשֶׂיךָ.
מַלְכוּתְךָ מַלְכוּת כָּל עֹלָמִים, וּמֶמְשַׁלְתְּךָ בְּכָל דּוֹר וָדוֹר.
יְהוָֹה מֶלֶךְ, יְהוָֹה מָלָךְ, יְהוָֹה יִמְלֹךְ לְעוֹלָם וָעֶד.

Avinu Malkeinu

j. אָבִינוּ מַלְכֵּנוּ, חָנֵּנוּ וַעֲנֵנוּ, כִּי אֵין בָּנוּ
מַעֲשִׂים, עֲשֵׂה עִמָּנוּ צְדָקָה וָחֶסֶד וְהוֹשִׁיעֵנוּ.

V'al Kulam

k. וְעַל כֻּלָּם אֱלוֹהַּ סְלִיחוֹת, סְלַח לָנוּ, מְחַל לָנוּ, כַּפֶּר לָנוּ.

From the *Kaddish*

l. יִתְבָּרַךְ וְיִשְׁתַּבַּח, וְיִתְפָּאַר וְיִתְרוֹמַם
וְיִתְנַשֵּׂא, וְיִתְהַדָּר וְיִתְעַלֶּה וְיִתְהַלָּל
שְׁמֵהּ דְּקֻדְשָׁא, בְּרִיךְ הוּא, לְעֵלָּא מִן
כָּל בִּרְכָתָא וְשִׁירָתָא, תֻּשְׁבְּחָתָא
וְנֶחֱמָתָא דַּאֲמִירָן בְּעָלְמָא, וְאִמְרוּ אָמֵן.

EXTRA CREDIT

"Doing" and "Hearing"

You have already encountered the Hebrew root שׁ-מ-ע in the vocabulary word שְׁמַע, which was introduced in Chapter 4. The root שׁ-מ-ע has the basic meaning of "hear" or "listen" or "obey." In this chapter, you were introduced to the Hebrew root ע-שׂ-ה, which has the basic meaning of "make" or "do" or "act." Both of these roots appear in the following biblical verse, which relates the response of the Children of Israel after the Revelation of the Torah at Mt. Sinai:

וַיֹּאמְרוּ כֹּל אֲשֶׁר דִּבֶּר יְהֹוָה נַעֲשֶׂה וְנִשְׁמָע.

And they said: "All that the Eternal has spoken, we will do and we will obey." (Exodus 24:7)

Many commentaries on this verse focus on the interpretation of the words נַעֲשֶׂה וְנִשְׁמָע, translated above as "we will do and we will obey." It is, however, also possible to understand these words as "we will act and we will hear," or even as "we will act, then we will hear." With such an interpretation, the sequence of the two verbs in the verse is noteworthy, for their order seems to be backwards: doesn't one *first* hear a command and *then* act upon it?

The fact that the Children of Israel responded in this manner is generally interpreted as a sign of their willingness to accept the Torah. Before even hearing all the details, they were already prepared to commit themselves to action. The following midrash reflects this point of view:

One whose good deeds exceed his learning, his learning will endure. But one whose learning exceeds his good deeds, his learning will not endure. For it is said נַעֲשֶׂה, "we will act" (i.e., we will do good deeds), וְנִשְׁמָע, "then we will hear" (i.e., then we will learn). (*Avot D'Rabbi Natan* 22)

Review

You have now learned the following Hebrew letters.

שׁ ב ת ל מ ם ס ה ר א ע נ ן

ח כ ך ו ב צ ץ ד י כ ק פּ

שׂ ס פ ף

You have learned eighteen vowel symbols.

You have learned the irregular ending הַ.

And you have learned fourteen basic Jewish vocabulary words.

שַׁבָּת שָׁלוֹם תּוֹרָה שֵׁם שְׁמַע

בָּרוּךְ בְּרָכָה תְּשׁוּבָה אַהֲבָה

מִצְוָה חַיִּים צְדָקָה תְּפִלָּה שִׂמְחָה

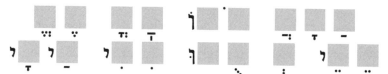

rest, cease from labor, desist	—	שׁ-ב-ת
complete, whole	—	שׁ-ל-ם
guard, keep, preserve	—	שׁ-מ-ר
give, grant, permit	—	נ-ת-ן
bless	—	ב-ר-ך
love, affection	—	א-ה-ב
command, order	—	צ-ו-ה
holy, sacred, set apart	—	ק-ד-שׁ
make, do, act	—	ע-שׂ-ה

This chapter introduces three new letters. One of them, the letter *Tet*, has the same sound as the letter *Tav* introduced in Chapter 1.

Gimmel	**g** as in **g**ood	ג
Tet	**t** as in **t**ie	ט
Zayin	**z** as in **z**ebra	ז

Look-Alike Letters

The letters *Gimmel* and *Nun* are similar in appearance, but the *Nun* has a solid horizontal bar across the bottom while the *Gimmel* has a gap in its bottom horizontal bar, forming a tail at the bottom right corner of the letter. You might remember this difference by noting that the letter *Gimmel*, which sounds like *g*, has a **g**ap.

The letters *Tet* and *Mem* also look very much alike. Notice, however, that the letter *Tet* has an opening at the top, while the letter *Mem* has an opening at the bottom. You might remember this difference by thinking that the letter *Tet*, which sounds like *t*, is like a **t**eapot letting the steam escape from its opening above, while the letter *Mem*, which sounds like *m*, is like a **m**olehill, with a little opening underneath for the mole to enter.

The letters *Zayin* and *Vav* also are very similar in appearance. The *Zayin*, however, is formed from two distinct lines: a short top bar and a vertical line that descends from the middle of the top bar. The *Vav* is formed from one continuous line with a curved hook at the top.

The letters *Zayin* and *Nun Sofit* also look alike. The *Zayin*, however, is shorter than the *Nun Sofit*, which drops down below the line of print. The letter *Zayin* can appear anywhere in a word, while the *Nun Sofit* can appear only as a final letter.

ז ן

Reading Practice

Say aloud the sounds of the following letters, which include some from previous chapters as well as the new letters. Try to do this without looking at the chart on the preceding page.

.a   ז ו ז ז ן ז ו נ ג כ נ ג נ ג

.b   ט מ כ ט ק ט ס מ ס מ ט מ ט

.c   ז ו ט מ ס פ ף פ ך ב כ נ ג

.d   מ ט ד ר כ נ ו ז י ת ח ה

Read aloud the following letter and vowel combinations.

.e   גוֹ נוֹ נוּ גֻ גֵי טַ זִי וִי זְ וֶ זָ גֶ נְ

.f   טִי מַי גֵי גֻ טֻ טָ מֶ וַ זַ זוּ טוּ מֹ

.g   גוּ גֶ נֵי נִי גִי זִ וֹ זוֹ זָ טַ טֶ טִ

Read aloud the following single-syllable combinations.

.h   בֵז כֵז נֵז גֵז טֹז גֹז טוּז מוּז מֵז טֵז

.i   צֵיט אָט אָם רֵט דֵט הֵט חוּט סֵט

.j   שִׂיג שׂגַ פֵּג סוֹג טוֹג טוֹב מוֹב

.k   זֵף זִיו זָף זֶף זֶט זֵץ זֹס וֹס נֹשׂ גֹשׂ

Read aloud the following longer combinations of letters and vowels.

.l   גֵּנֵב גְּנֵז גֹּנֵן גֹּסֵס גֹּרֵס גָּרֵם גָּרֵף

.m   גוֹמֵל גוֹלֵל זוֹלֵל זוֹלֵג זֹלֵף יִזְלֹף זַלֵף

.n   טֶרֶם טָרֵף בֶּטֶן בֶּטַח טָבַח טֶבַע

.o   טִפָּה הֵטָה הֵטִיל הֵטִיף לֵטֹף שָׁטֹף

.p   זוֹרֵחַ בּוֹטֵחַ בָּטוּחַ נָטוּעַ גָזוּל גָּמֵץ גֵּיץ

.q   אַזֵכֶּה אֲגָאָה אֲפֵנֵג מְפִיג יְפַלֵג יְקַלְגֵּס

.r   הֶאֱזִין הֵעֱזִיר הִזְדַּמֵּן הִצְטָרֵךְ הִסְתַּדֵּר

You have learned the letters and vowels that form the Hebrew root ט-ו-ב. The basic meaning of this root is "good," and from it are derived two common Jewish vocabulary words:

טוֹב and טוֹבָה

Each of these words can be used as an adjective or a noun and so can be translated as either "good" or "goodness." (The word טוֹב can also be used as the adverb "well.") In addition, these words may be translated into English in a variety of different ways depending on the context, such as the adjectives "fair," "pleasant," "fine," and "kind," or the nouns "fairness," "favor," "kindness," "good deed," and "virtue."

HEBREW Key Quote

Numbers 24:5 and Psalm 133:1

A form of the root ט-ו-ב appears in each of the following biblical verses. Numbers 24, verse 5, appears in the prayer book at the opening of daily, Shabbat, and festival services. Verse 1 of Psalm 133, set to music, has become a well-known Hebrew folk song. It is also sometimes incorporated into liturgical settings.

מַה טֹּבוּ אֹהָלֶיךָ יַעֲקֹב מִשְׁכְּנֹתֶיךָ יִשְׂרָאֵל.

How fair are your tents, O Jacob, your dwellings, O Israel! (Numbers 24:5)

הִנֵּה מַה טּוֹב וּמַה נָּעִים שֶׁבֶת אַחִים גַּם־יָחַד.

How good and how pleasant it is when brothers and sisters dwell together (Psalm 133:1)

You have learned all of the Hebrew vowel symbols. In this chapter, we introduce two vowel sounds that appear only infrequently in the prayer book and in the Bible. These two sounds are formed by placing the letter *Yod* after the וֹ and the וּ vowels.

sounds like **oy** as in **toy**	וֹי
sounds like **ooey** as in **gooey**	וּי

Reading Practice

Read aloud the following letter and vowel combinations.

אוֹי גּוֹי שׁוֹי נוֹי סוֹי בּוֹי פּוֹי הוֹי .a

קוּי לוּי וּוִי שׁוּי רוּי תּוּי חוּי צוּי .b

אוֹיָה אוֹיֵב עוֹיֵן עוֹינוֹת גּוֹיֵי גּוֹיִים .c

מָצוּי רָאוּי נָטוּי עָשׂוּי גְּלוּי שְׁנוּי .d

You have now learned the letters that form a very common Hebrew root: ז-כ-ר. This root has the basic meaning of "remember." It appears frequently in the prayer book and in the Bible.

Following are examples of Hebrew words formed from the root ז-כ-ר.

memorable	—	זָכִיר
remembrance	—	זְכִירָה
Yizkor (memorial prayer)	—	יִזְכֹּר
mentioning, reminding, recalling to memory	—	הַזְכָּרָה
secretary	—	מַזְכִּיר
souvenir, reminder	—	מַזְכֶּרֶת
memory, remembrance; trace, hint	—	זֵכֶר
in memory of	—	לְזֵכֶר
memory, remembrance, commemoration	—	זִכָּרוֹן
mnemonics	—	זִכְרוֹנִיּוֹת
forget-me-not (plant)	—	זִכְרִינִי
Zechariah	—	זְכַרְיָה

Try to find the root ז-כ-ר in each of the following prayer book excerpts. The number of occurrences of the root in each excerpt is indicated in parentheses. In most cases, prefixes and/or suffixes are attached.

L'ma-an Tizk'ru (Numbers 15:40) (1 occurrence)

לְמַעַן תִּזְכְּרוּ וַעֲשִׂיתֶם אֶת כָּל מִצְוֹתָי וִהְיִיתֶם קְדֹשִׁים לֵאלֹהֵיכֶם.

Shabbat evening Kiddush (2 occurrences)

בָּרוּךְ אַתָּה יְיָ אֱלֹהֵינוּ מֶלֶךְ הָעוֹלָם, אֲשֶׁר קִדְּשָׁנוּ בְּמִצְוֹתָיו וְרָצָה בָנוּ, וְשַׁבַּת קָדְשׁוֹ בְּאַהֲבָה וּבְרָצוֹן הִנְחִילָנוּ, זִכָּרוֹן לְמַעֲשֵׂה בְרֵאשִׁית. כִּי הוּא יוֹם תְּחִלָּה לְמִקְרָאֵי קֹדֶשׁ, זֵכֶר לִיצִיאַת מִצְרָיִם.

From Yism'chu (1 occurrence)

וְהַשְּׁבִיעִי רָצִיתָ בּוֹ וְקִדַּשְׁתּוֹ, חֶמְדַּת יָמִים אוֹתוֹ קָרָאתָ, זֵכֶר לְמַעֲשֵׂה בְרֵאשִׁית.

High Holy Day addition to the Amidah (1 occurrence)

זָכְרֵנוּ לְחַיִּים, מֶלֶךְ חָפֵץ בַּחַיִּים, וְכָתְבֵנוּ בְּסֵפֶר הַחַיִּים, לְמַעַנְךָ אֱלֹהִים חַיִּים.

Yaaleh V'yavo (4 occurrences)

אֱלֹהֵינוּ וֵאלֹהֵי אֲבוֹתֵינוּ וְאִמּוֹתֵינוּ, יַעֲלֶה וְיָבֹא, וְיִזָּכֵר זִכְרוֹנֵנוּ וְזִכְרוֹן כָּל עַמְּךָ בֵּית יִשְׂרָאֵל לְפָנֶיךָ, לְטוֹבָה, לְחֵן, לְחֶסֶד, וּלְרַחֲמִים, לְחַיִּים וּלְשָׁלוֹם, בְּיוֹם

לְרֹאשׁ־חֹדֶשׁ:   רֹאשׁ הַחֹדֶשׁ הַזֶּה.

לְפֶסַח: חַג הַמַּצּוֹת הַזֶּה.

לְסֻכּוֹת: חַג הַסֻּכּוֹת הַזֶּה.

זָכְרֵנוּ, יְיָ, אֱלֹהֵינוּ, בּוֹ לְטוֹבָה.

These are the block print forms of the Hebrew letters introduced in this chapter.

ז זֵ טֻ טֹ גֶּ גֵּ

These are their script forms.

פֿ זֵ טֻ טֹ גֶּ גֵּ

The script forms of the letters *Zayin* and *Gimmel* are mirror images of one another. You can remember which one is the letter *Gimmel* by noting that the curve of this letter, which sounds like *g*, faces the same direction as the curve of a capital letter *G*.

Hebrew Writing Exercises

1. Write a line of the letter *Gimmel*, using either block print or script.

ג _____

2. Write a line of the letter *Tet*, using either block print or script.

ט _____

3. Write a line of the letter *Zayin*, using either block print or script.

ז _____

Exercises

1. Draw a line connecting each Hebrew consonant and vowel combination with the English word that has the same sound.

gaze	גִּיס	tock	פוּי
tease	מֵט	haze	רֵג
geese	טִיא	phooey	טָק
ghoul	זוֹן	pet	דוֹז
tie	רֵז	rogue	סוֹי
ruse	טִיז	goose	הֵז

met	גֶז	doze	גוֹש
zone	גוּל	soy	פֶּט

2. The following Hebrew combinations sound like real English words in sentences. Read aloud.

רוֹי סֶד טוּ בַּב: "אַי פִּיל יֶר פֵּין."

בַּב סֶד: "נֹה יוּ דוּ נַט!

מֵי פִּיט אֵיק!

מֵי טוֹז אֵיק!

מֵי נִיז אֵיק!

מֵי אַיז אֵיק!

יוּ דוּ נַט פִּיל מֵי אֵיק!"

"אוֹי וֵי!" סֶד רוֹי.

3. Write the Hebrew consonant and vowel combinations that sound like the following English words. There is more than one possibility for each word.

a. coy _____

b. toy _____

c. tomb _____

_____ _____ _____

d. zoom _____

e. get _____

f. gate _____

_____ _____ _____

g. gaze _____

h. goes _____

i. mows _____

_____ _____ _____

j. zeal _____

k. keys _____

l. cog _____

_____ _____ _____

4. The following reading practice focuses on look-alike letters that can be easily confused. Read each combination aloud.

זִיז זִיו זַיִן זַוִּין זוּף זְוַוג זִינָה זָנָב a.

מִטָּה טְפָה טִיבָה מִיכָה טִימָה b.

גְּעָרוֹת נְעָרוֹת גְּעָדוֹת וְעָדוֹת נֶעְדָּר c.

Try to read the following words and phrases in Hebrew first to see if you recognize them before looking at the English translation.

Haggadah (saga, telling, retelling)	—	הַגָּדָה
mezuzah, doorpost	—	מְזוּזָה
prayer shawl	—	טַלִּית
Oneg Shabbat (*literally:* enjoyment of Shabbat)	—	עֹנֶג שַׁבָּת
Tu Bish'vat	—	טוּ בִּשְׁבָט
cycle, festival prayer book	—	מַחֲזוֹר
Grace after Meals	—	בִּרְכַּת הַמָּזוֹן
etrog, citron	—	אֶתְרוֹג
divorce	—	גֵּט
Gemara	—	גְּמָרָא
nation, people (also used to refer to a non-Jew)	—	גּוֹי
Happy New Year (*literally:* a good year)	—	שָׁנָה טוֹבָה
good morning	—	בֹּקֶר טוֹב
good night	—	לַיְלָה טוֹב
a good week (greeting upon the conclusion of Shabbat)	—	שָׁבוּעַ טוֹב
the good inclination	—	יֵצֶר הַטּוֹב
good deeds	—	מַעֲשִׂים טוֹבִים

CHAPTER 10

5. Read aloud the following letter and vowel combinations.

a. סוֹיָה גּוֹיָה גּוֹרֵס גּוֹרֵם כּוֹרֵם שׁוֹטֵם

b. שֶׁלֶג פֶּלֶג סֶרֶט סֶרֶן קֶרֶן קֶרֶשׁ

c. בָּנוּי הַבָּנוּי רָצוּי וְרָצוּי וְקָלוּי וּגְלוּיָה

d. מִגְדָּל מִזְמֹר מִטְבָּח מִזְבֵּחַ מַטְבֵּחַ

e. זְכוּכִית זְחִיחוּת זְהִירוּת זְקִיפוּת

f. הֶחֱזִיר הֶחֱזִיק הֶחֱוִיר הֶחֱיָה הֶחֱטִיא

g. אֲגִיץ אֲגִיף אֲנָזֶף אֲזַנַּח אֲגָנַח אֲגְנֵז

h. יִצְטָרֵד יִצְטָרֵךְ יִצְטָרֵף יִצְטַמֵּק

i. הִזְדַּנֵּב הִזְדַּוֵּג הִזְדַּעֵף הִזְדָּרֵז הִזְדַּקֵּר

6. The following excerpts from the Bible or the prayer book all contain a word with either the
וֹי or the וִי vowel sound. Read aloud.

From the *Aleinu*

a. עָלֵינוּ לְשַׁבֵּחַ לַאֲדוֹן הַכֹּל, לָתֵת גְּדֻלָּה
לְיוֹצֵר בְּרֵאשִׁית, שֶׁלֹּא עָשָׂנוּ כְּגוֹיֵי
הָאֲרָצוֹת, וְלֹא שָׂמָנוּ כְּמִשְׁפְּחוֹת הָאֲדָמָה...

From *Hashkiveinu*

b. הַשְׁכִּיבֵנוּ יְיָ אֱלֹהֵינוּ לְשָׁלוֹם, וְהַעֲמִידֵנוּ
מַלְכֵּנוּ לְחַיִּים. וּפְרוֹשׂ עָלֵינוּ סֻכַּת שְׁלוֹמֶךָ,
וְתַקְּנֵנוּ בְּעֵצָה טוֹבָה מִלְּפָנֶיךָ, וְהוֹשִׁיעֵנוּ
לְמַעַן שְׁמֶךָ, וְהָגֵן בַּעֲדֵנוּ, וְהָסֵר מֵעָלֵינוּ
אוֹיֵב, דֶּבֶר, וְחֶרֶב, וְרָעָב וְיָגוֹן...

Isaiah 2:4; Micah 4:3

c. לֹא יִשָּׂא גוֹי אֶל גּוֹי חֶרֶב וְלֹא יִלְמְדוּ עוֹד מִלְחָמָה.

Song of Songs 4:4

d. כְּמִגְדַּל דָּוִיד צַוָּארֵךְ בָּנוּי לְתַלְפִּיּוֹת...

Exodus 3:16

e. פָּקֹד פָּקַדְתִּי אֶתְכֶם וְאֶת הֶעָשׂוּי לָכֶם בְּמִצְרָיִם.

7. The following prayer book excerpts all contain at least one of the new letters (ט, ז, and ג) introduced in this chapter. Read aloud.

From the Passover Haggadah's Four Questions

a. מַה נִּשְׁתַּנָּה הַלַּיְלָה הַזֶּה מִכָּל הַלֵּילוֹת?

Blessing over wine or grape juice

b. בָּרוּךְ אַתָּה יְיָ אֱלֹהֵינוּ מֶלֶךְ הָעוֹלָם,
בּוֹרֵא פְּרִי הַגָּפֶן.

From *Adon Olam*

c. אֲדוֹן עוֹלָם אֲשֶׁר מָלַךְ, בְּטֶרֶם כָּל יְצִיר נִבְרָא.
לְעֵת נַעֲשָׂה בְחֶפְצוֹ כֹּל, אֲזַי מֶלֶךְ שְׁמוֹ נִקְרָא.

From *V'ahavta* (Deuteronomy 6:8–9)

d. וּקְשַׁרְתָּם לְאוֹת עַל יָדֶךָ, וְהָיוּ לְטֹטָפֹת
בֵּין עֵינֶיךָ, וּכְתַבְתָּם עַל מְזֻזוֹת בֵּיתֶךָ וּבִשְׁעָרֶיךָ.

From *L'chah Dodi*

e. שָׁמוֹר וְזָכוֹר בְּדִבּוּר אֶחָד, הִשְׁמִיעָנוּ אֵל
הַמְּיֻחָד. יְיָ אֶחָד וּשְׁמוֹ אֶחָד, לְשֵׁם
וּלְתִפְאֶרֶת וְלִתְהִלָּה.

From *G'vurot*

f. אַתָּה גִּבּוֹר לְעוֹלָם אֲדֹנָי, מְחַיֵּה הַכֹּל אַתָּה, רַב לְהוֹשִׁיעַ.

From the Shabbat Psalm (Psalm 92:1–2)

g. מִזְמוֹר שִׁיר לְיוֹם הַשַּׁבָּת: טוֹב לְהֹדוֹת
לַיהוָה וּלְזַמֵּר לְשִׁמְךָ עֶלְיוֹן.

Yihyu L'ratzon (Psalm 19:15)

h. יִהְיוּ לְרָצוֹן אִמְרֵי פִי וְהֶגְיוֹן לִבִּי לְפָנֶיךָ, יְיָ צוּרִי וְגוֹאֲלִי.

From the Torah service (I Chronicles 29:11)

i. לְךָ יְהוָה הַגְּדֻלָּה וְהַגְּבוּרָה וְהַתִּפְאֶרֶת
וְהַנֵּצַח וְהַהוֹד, כִּי כֹל בַּשָּׁמַיִם
וּבָאָרֶץ, לְךָ יְהוָה הַמַּמְלָכָה וְהַמִּתְנַשֵּׂא לְכֹל לְרֹאשׁ.

Meditation before the *Avot* (Psalm 51:17)

j. אֲדֹנָי שְׂפָתַי תִּפְתָּח וּפִי יַגִּיד תְּהִלָּתֶךָ.

From *Sim Shalom*

k. שִׂים שָׁלוֹם טוֹבָה וּבְרָכָה, חֵן וָחֶסֶד
וְרַחֲמִים, עָלֵינוּ וְעַל כָּל יִשְׂרָאֵל עַמֶּךָ.

Avot

l. בָּרוּךְ אַתָּה יְיָ אֱלֹהֵינוּ וֵאלֹהֵי אֲבוֹתֵינוּ
וְאִמּוֹתֵינוּ: אֱלֹהֵי אַבְרָהָם, אֱלֹהֵי יִצְחָק,
וֵאלֹהֵי יַעֲקֹב. אֱלֹהֵי שָׂרָה, אֱלֹהֵי רִבְקָה,
אֱלֹהֵי לֵאָה וֵאלֹהֵי רָחֵל. הָאֵל הַגָּדוֹל
הַגִּבּוֹר וְהַנּוֹרָא, אֵל עֶלְיוֹן, גּוֹמֵל חֲסָדִים
טוֹבִים, וְקוֹנֵה הַכֹּל, וְזוֹכֵר חַסְדֵי אָבוֹת
וְאִמָּהוֹת, וּמֵבִיא גְאֻלָּה לִבְנֵי בְנֵיהֶם,
לְמַעַן שְׁמוֹ בְּאַהֲבָה. מֶלֶךְ עוֹזֵר וּמוֹשִׁיעַ
וּמָגֵן. בָּרוּךְ אַתָּה יְיָ, מָגֵן אַבְרָהָם וְעֶזְרַת שָׂרָה.

In Conclusion: A Blessing and an Exclamation

EXTRA CREDIT

You have reached the end of this book and have achieved a significant goal: learning all the letters and vowels of the Hebrew alphabet. There is a Hebrew blessing that is appropriate for this occasion, a blessing that acknowledges the Divine Presence in our lives, sustaining us and enabling us to reach special times of joy or accomplishment. This blessing is said, for example, at the beginning of festivals, when lighting the first Chanukah candle, when hearing the shofar sounded on Rosh HaShanah, when tasting a fruit for the first time in the season, when putting on a new garment, and when moving into a new home. Some families say it at family reunions or at other significant events in their home lives. You may wish to say it aloud now, as you celebrate the conclusion of this stage of your Hebrew study and the beginning of the next.

בָּרוּךְ אַתָּה יְיָ אֱלֹהֵינוּ מֶלֶךְ הָעוֹלָם, שֶׁהֶחֱיָנוּ וְקִיְּמָנוּ וְהִגִּיעָנוּ לַזְּמַן הַזֶּה.

Vuhegeanu   *Vakeeymanu*   *shechecheeanu*   *huzeh*   *iuzman*

Blessed are You, Eternal our God, Sovereign of the universe, who has given us life and sustained us and enabled us to reach this time.

In addition, there is a well-known Hebrew exclamation that is appropriate for this moment. This exclamation uses the word טוֹב, introduced in this chapter, which means "good." It also uses the word מַזָּל, which originally meant a "planet" or a "constellation." A מַזָּל טוֹב was a "good constellation," a lucky sign in the heavens. Hence, the word מַזָּל came to mean "luck," and the expression מַזָּל טוֹב to mean "good luck." This expression is used like the English exclamation "congratulations!"—to express pleasure and good wishes on the occasion of another's fortune or success. And so, we conclude with this statement to you:

מַזָּל טוֹב!

For Further Jewish Learning

Bronstein, Herbert, ed. *A Passover Haggadah: The New Union Haggadah.* New York: CCAR, 1974.

Elkins, Dov Peretz. *A Shabbat Reader: Universe of Cosmic Joy.* New York: UAHC Press, 1999.

Falk, Marcia. *Book of Blessings: A New Prayer Book for the Weekdays, the Sabbath, and the New Moon Festival.* San Francisco: Harper San Francisco, 1996.

Hoffman, Lawrence A., ed. *My People's Prayer Book: Traditional Prayers, Modern Commentaries: The Sh'ma and Its Blessings.* Woodstock, Vermont: Jewish Lights Publishing, 1997.

Hoffman, Lawrence A., ed. *My People's Prayer Book: Traditional Prayers, Modern Commentaries: The Amidah.* Woodstock, Vermont: Jewish Lights Publishing, 1998.

Hoffman, Lawrence A., ed. *My People's Prayer Book, Traditional Prayers, Modern Commentaries: P'Sukei D'Zimrah (Morning Psalms).* Woodstock, Vermont: Jewish Lights Publishing, 1999.

Kushner, Lawrence. *The Book of Letters: A Mystical Alef-Bait.* Woodstock, Vermont: Jewish Lights Publishing, 1991.

Kushner, Lawrence. *The Book of Words (Sefer Shel Devarim): Talking Spiritual Life, Living Spiritual Talk.* Woodstock, Vermont: Jewish Lights Publishing, 1993.

Perelson, Ruth. *An Invitation to Shabbat: A Beginner's Guide to Weekly Celebration.* New York: UAHC Press, 1997.

Plaut, W. Gunther, ed. *Torah: A Modern Commentary.* New York: UAHC Press, 1981.

Plaut, W. Gunther, ed. *The Haftarah Commentary.* New York: UAHC Press, 1998.

Stern, Chaim, ed. *Gates of Prayer: The New Union Prayerbook.* New York: CCAR Press, 1975.

Stern, Chaim, ed. *Gates of Repentance: The New Union Prayerbook for the Days of Awe.* New York: CCAR Press, 1978.

Stern, Chaim, ed. *Gates of Prayer for Shabbat and Weekdays: A Gender Sensitive Prayerbook.* New York: CCAR Press, 1994.

Stern, Chaim, ed. *On the Doorposts of Your House: Prayers and Ceremonies for the Jewish Home.* New York: CCAR Press, 1994.

Syme, Daniel B. *The Jewish Home: A Guide for Jewish Living.* New York: UAHC Press, 1988.

Further Hebrew Resources

Motzkin, Linda. *Aleph Isn't Enough: An Introduction to Hebrew for Adults, Book II.* New York: UAHC Press, 2001.

THIS BOOK IS ORGANIZED AROUND WELL-KNOWN PASSAGES FROM THE PRAYERBOOK AND BIBLE AND INCLUDES FURTHER READING PRACTICE FOR THOSE WHO HAVE FINISHED ALEPH ISN'T TOUGH. IT PROVIDES EXPLANATIONS OF BASIC HEBREW LANGUAGE STRUCTURES, ROOTS AND VOCABULARY, WHICH APPEAR IN THE PRAYERBOOK AND BIBLICAL PASSAGES SELECTED. EACH CHAPTER INCLUDES ADDITIONAL INFORMATION ON A TOPIC RELATED TO HEBREW LANGUAGE OR JEWISH LIFE. ALL MATERIAL IS PRESENTED IN A CLEAR AND SIMPLE WAY. TEN CHAPTERS.

Anderson, Motzkin, Rubenstein and Wiseman. *Prayerbook Hebrew: The Easy Way.* Oakland, California: EKS Publishing Co., 1985

THIS BOOK PRESENTS BASIC GRAMMAR AND PRAYERBOOK HEBREW VOCABULARY IN RELATIVELY SIMPLE, CLEAR LANGUAGE. IT IS ORGANIZED AROUND GRAMMATICAL CONCEPTS, WITH EACH CHAPTER CONCLUDING WITH A WELL-KNOWN HEBREW PRAYER ILLUSTRATING THE CONCEPTS INTRODUCED. TWENTY ONE CHAPTERS.

Simon, Resnikoff, Motzkin. *The First Hebrew Primer: the Adult Beginner's Path to Biblical Hebrew.* Oakland, California: EKS Publishing Co., 1992

THIS BOOK IS A COMPREHENSIVE BIBLICAL HEBREW GRAMMAR, WRITTEN IN NON-TECHNICAL LANGUAGE. IT IS USED IN MANY COLLEGES AND SEMINARIES, IN ADDITION TO SYNAGOGUE CLASSES, AS AN INTRODUCTION TO BIBLICAL HEBREW. THIRTY CHAPTERS.

The following books are the standard references on the technical aspects of classical Hebrew grammar.

Greenberg, Moshe. *Introduction to Hebrew.* Englewood Cliffs, New Jersey: Prentice-Hall, Inc., 1965.

Lambdin, Thomas O. *Introduction to Biblical Hebrew.* New York: Charles Scribner's Sons, 1971

Weingreen, Jacob. *A Practical Grammar for Classical Hebrew.* London: Oxford University Press, 1959.